P9-DCZ-842

To order additional books at a
discount over major retailers go to:

www.cooperpest.com

and click on WOW! Site

WHAT + HOW = WOW

WHAT + HOW = WOW

Phillip Cooper

To order additional copies of this book, contact:
Xlibris Corporation
1-888-795-4274
www.Xlibris.com
Orders@Xlibris.com
19829

CONTENTS

To Passion.
Passion for my family, friends and life...
For all that was, all that is,
and all that is yet to come.

Acknowledgements

WOW was a concept I stumbled into and it has changed my life. The book is the culmination of my experiences with WOW and so many people have been instrumental in its success.

Without the motivational force of my wife Laura none of this would be possible. She is my inspiration for all of the things I am able to accomplish, and I only hope to give her in return what she gives me. My kids, Samantha and Andrew are a big part of the WOW story. Samantha has been with me on WOW since she was five, when she started grading tapes with me. She is some kind of kid. I thank Andrew for providing the necessary distractions in my headstrong moments.

My brother, and business partner Rick, pushed me to introduce WOW to Cooper Pest Control and never stopped prodding me along the way of completing this book. I have the best brother one could have. He has and continues to push me to greater heights and I know we make a great team. Thanks to my sister-in-law Louise and my nieces Julia and Andrea for allowing Rick to be part of the special Cooper Pest Control story.

My other family is my team at Cooper Pest Control, Inc. They have been great through the entire process. Robin Morgan and Nancy Kintner have lived WOW since its inception and I am eternally indebted to them for their tireless efforts on my behalf. Thanks also to Lauren Brown for insuring that we found the time in my busy schedule to complete the book. The three of them are the best. There are so many others at our remarkable company who have made this possible and to all of you, I love coming to work everyday for all of the things that you bring to the table. It is through your hard work and perseverance that WOW is a reality and is alive and well.

WOW would not be what it is today without the inspiration of Bob Palestri and Mike Amoroso who saw an in-house program and realized the potential for customer service organizations world-wide. Bob and Mike are the genesis of what WOW is today. They loaded the bases and provided an opportunity for a WOW moment and the result is this book.

There are so many companies that are part of this book but special thoughts go to Deb Jacovelli and John Manning at Commerce Bank for allowing me to get an insider's view of the bank; The Gale Company for striving for WOW. To Mike Ayars, of Marathon Data for providing open access to his entire staff and for providing the ability to watch his team in action.

My trials and tribulations along with incredible opportunities were part of my frequent five a.m conversations with my very good friend, Kurt Padavano, from Advance Realty. (we both start our days around four a.m.). Kurt helped me keep the faith as the book progressed. Kurt, I know that your book is next and I will be there for you.

To the Stepping Stone Bed & Breakfast in Stockton, NJ and their wonderful inn keepers Rick and Paula Baxter for providing a perfect setting when I need a jump start in my writing. Thank you for letting me bend your ear about my trials and tribulations, it was cleansing and allowed me to re-focus.

To Amy Goodwin, who I have not seen in 22 years, your lessons in English Comp classes at The George Washington University kept coming back as my editors delivered their comments. I know there are parts of the book that you would still red-line but I owe you so much for giving me the inspiration to communicate effectively. You forever changed my writing style and without you I doubt this book would have ever occurred.

When I started the book, I was confident it would be a snap. How humbling an experience this book has been. I learned how much grammar I forgot over the years. Writing emails and internal correspondence, and writing a book are two different ball games. Ultimately, the completion of the book was a team effort. I had the best review and editing team a person could have. These guys, and ladies, are the best: Jerry Mix, Kevin Wheeler, Susan Franuberger, Lorraine Kucinski, John Dinsmore and Dawn Liles; I will be forever remember your tireless efforts in making the book what it is. To Judy Dold, thank you for being tough on me, the best criticism is the toughest to swallow.

My final draft editor, Len Vermillion stepped to the plate to insure a product worthy of print.

To, Rachel Stark, who is the best legal counsel and friend a guy could have, thank you for talking through all of the concerns I had regarding publishing this work.

For one and a half years, every Friday night, my Pizza Friday crew listened to my progress reports. How tiring it must have become. To the best neighbors a family could have Kevin and Kim DeLaney; Bill and Daryl Baldwin; Rob and Kim McFadden; Kevin and Jane Young and Dave and Susanne Vaughan, it is finally done!

And most important of all, none of this would be possible without my mom and dad. To dad, I am sorry you are not here to see what you started but I know you are reading the book upstairs. There were many times during the process that I heard your comments from up high and I always listened. To mom, your imprints are throughout the book, the book is a testimony to all of your hard work in making me what I am today. I will be eternally grateful for all you have done. You loaded the bases and gave me an opportunity to go for that WOW moment. Thank you.

PREFACE

WOW

Why WOW is important

Communication is the foundation of both our personal and professional lives. In 1997 I recognized my company, needed a change in the philosophy surrounding our methods of communication. Our customer service by many standards was above average, but in my estimation was nothing better than mediocre. As a result, we began the process of changing the way we communicate with our clients and it has transformed our company from one with merely single digit growth to one now growing by double digits, all the while increasing our profitability.

This book is for anyone who communicates, which is everyone. It will assist organizations to develop the means for their team members to improve their communication skills. It will guide individuals to take control of their destinies and provide a framework for developing superior customer relation skills.

WHAT + HOW = WOW is a method of practicing excellent communication, which is the cornerstone for every single action we perform. By utilizing the

WHAT + HOW methodology, a framework for future development is set in place. For those with a passion for excellence, WOW experiences will follow and it is the WOW experience that ultimately is the yardstick for success. The WOW moment is a special place in time when the impact of your actions has the other person so excited they cannot stop speaking about the experience. It is the WOW moment that all customer service professionals strive for and WHAT + HOW = WOW provides the framework for achieving WOW moments on a consistent basis.

Implementing WHAT + HOW is a serious investment for a company or an individual. It takes a great deal of practice to make it work, but when WOW is mastered it can lead to a hefty return on investment. There is much practice and commitment that the parties need to make.

Return on Investment

I find it exhilarating to see companies striving for the WOW moment, delivering outstanding communication to both their internal clients (teammates) and external clients (who they are delivering their product or service to). It is so exciting to see the results of successful WHAT + HOW implementation. The companies that have integrated the concepts of this book into their company's routines have:

- ➢ *Enhanced the communication process between teammates*
- ➢ *Increased their employee morale*
- ➢ *Improved sales by finding new opportunities*
- ➢ *Increased bottom line*

WHAT + HOW is a Passion

I practice what I preach. Later you will learn about taping and grading yourself. This is something I do on a weekly basis to maintain an edge. I am passionate about this topic because I know what it can do for organizations. My greatest satisfaction is going back to companies with which I have previously worked for and seeing them implement WOW and achieving extraordinary results. I love to sit down with their teammates who have gone through this program and learn how they have integrated it into their daily routines. Even more exciting is to see how it is enhancing the careers or each individual and how that translates into increasing their company's bottom line.

If you have the dedication and the guts to WOW, it can become your passion also and with it will come monumental results. You too, can make WHAT + HOW a passion and part of your daily routine. Whether it is at work or at home, life is about communication and WHAT + HOW provides the framework for taking your communication to a new level.

Family-Owned Business to Large Corporations

The WOW system is not only for large corporations, but can and has been successfully implemented in the two-person family business. Throughout the book I use examples of organizations that have made a commitment to customer service. Some of these organizations include: Advance Realty, Commerce Bank, Springer Pest Solutions, The Gale Company, Rottler Pest Control, Valcourt Building Services, and Griffin Pest Control. All of these companies have implemented WOW to inspire their work forces and enhance their communication with their internal and external clients. Although I have worked with large organizations, much of my time has been spent helping small family-owned businesses gain the competitive advantage in utilizing communication. Hailing from a second-generation family-owned business, I understand the challenges faced by small businesses. Whether you are a large multi-national conglomerate or a small business the precepts of WHAT + HOW = WOW apply and can be successfully implemented into an organization. All it takes is an understanding of the process and a commitment to excellence and the result will be a consistent outstanding impression to your clients time after time.

Chapter 1

The Origins of WOW

The definition of WOW

Whenever I speak the first question I am asked is, "What is WOW, what does it stand for?" The letters W-O-W do not stand for anything, but put together they spell WOW and that is what communication is all about.

The Merriam-Webster dictionary defines WOW as, *"an exclamation of astonishment or admiration . . . a sensational success . . . to impress or excite greatly."*

I use a very simple definition when determining if we have achieved a WOW moment. My definition of WOW is quite different than Merriam-Webster's,

"WOW is achieved when the experience makes such an excellent impression with the receiving party that it is shared with family and friends. When striving for WOW, the by-product is an incredible experience, which impresses everyone with whom we come in contact."

This definition of WOW is the essence of this book. It is how we go about trying to achieve those WOW moments that is so important. How we communicate on a daily basis creates the number of opportunities we find to WOW each other. This is not limited to customer service; it is a form of communication—a way of life. But WOW is really not that simple.

The WOW moment

I liken WOW moments to a grand slam in baseball. When Barry Bonds steps to the plate he has a chance to hit a home run each time. Yet the opportunity to hit a Grand Slam only occurs if three runners are on base; when this opportunity presents itself the opportunity for WOW is present. If Barry Bonds hits a Grand Slam, he is guaranteed a highlight on the 11 o'clock evening edition of ESPN SportsCenter, but if he hits a home run the highlight may or may not be shown. The guaranteed spot on Sports Center is the equivalent of *"when the experience makes such an excellent impression with the receiving party that it is shared by family and friends."* The by-product is the home-run or simply getting on base. We do not want to strike out in our communication and if we practice our skills then we are often likely to be on base. This is the by-product portion of the definition, *"When striving for WOW, the by-product is an incredible experience, which impresses everyone with whom we come in contact."*

WOW is about finding those grand slam opportunities and seizing them when they arrive. WOW moments are rare. When they happen, the feeling of satisfaction is incredible!

I love WOW moments, but just as much I love the by-product. Striving for the WOW moment leads to one thing—outstanding customer service—that's what it is all about. And although the result is aimed at customer service the other result is a change in the way we communicate day to day in our daily lives. We notice things about communication styles we were never aware of and our ability to effectively communicate provides us with outstanding results in our daily lives.

WHAT + HOW gets us to those WOW moments that we should treasure and strive for in everything we do.

Bringing WOW to Cooper Pest Control

Cooper Pest Control was founded in 1955 by my father, Ted Cooper. My father instilled the belief that serving clients was critical and that the bar should always be high. Today, I own the company with my brother Richard, a leading entomologist in the country. Together, we have taken an incredible base our father left us and built it into one the of Top 100 pest management businesses, in terms of size, in the country. From a customer service perspective, I like to believe we are the tops in the country and still striving to get better.

It happens that we are in the pest management business, but our business is no different than any other service business. Our business is not about killing bugs, it is about satisfying clients and WOW helps us achieve this objective.

It was not always this way. When I arrived on the scene at Cooper in 1984 we had an excellent local reputation. Over the next 13 years we grew the company and were experiencing single-digit growth (3 percent-7 percent) and our profits were remaining flat. I was constantly looking for new opportunities to turn this into double-digit growth with increasing margins.

Although many ideas were attempted and had varying degrees of success, nothing made a substantial difference. In 1997, I turned my attention to the core activity of our business-customer service. I was not pleased with our level of customer service and I set about validating my beliefs. I added a customer service survey to our invoices expecting low scores to come back. The survey graded a number of questions on a 1 to 5 scale, 1=POOR, 2=BELOW AVEAGE 3=AVERAGE 4=ABOVE AVERAGE, 5=EXCELLENT. I expected scores of 2 or 3 and this was going to be my leverage to upgrade our level of customer service.

Surprisingly, the results came back overwhelmingly with 4s and 5s, customers said they were receiving above average to excellent customer service.

At first I was perplexed and then I stared examining my own customer service experiences. As I reviewed more, I recognized it was not that we were above average or excellent, but that the level of customer service our clients were exposed to in other parts of their lives was so poor. Our clients' standards had been lowered so greatly that our mediocre customer communication was excellent in their mind. As I started to examine other company's customer service departments it became apparent that customer service in general was pretty poor. The more companies I examined the less impressed I became. But the fact remained that in my opinion, our customer service at Cooper Pest Control was simply mediocre.

Just as interesting as the customers' impression of the Cooper Pest Control staff was our impression of ourselves. Our staff viewed themselves as delivering excellent customer service. They too had fallen into the mediocre trap and viewed their mediocre performance as very good customer service. This had to change and something radical was needed.

To elevate the level of customer service at Cooper I needed to find a methodology that my team could learn from. I knew there were some excellent customer service companies, but I was not sure how to capture their magic and implement it with my team. I started searching in my memory of all of the keynote speeches I had heard and books I had read on customer service. I looked at Nordstrom, L.L. Bean, American Express, Disney and other leaders in the world of customer service. I listened to many excellent speakers discuss the value of outstanding customer service and the principles that guided their companies in delivering excellent client relations. I read books preaching the values of customer service and highlighting organizations that delivered top-notch service. But each was missing the one ingredient I was looking for, a method to PRACTICE.

I kept thinking of professionals, including athletes, musicians and actors. Each practiced their trade and it was my conclusion that this was the missing piece. Each of these professions had identifiable skills that could be honed with the ultimate result of becoming outstanding in their fields. Each of these professions practiced their trade on a regular basis to be the best they could be. My teammates at Cooper had nothing to practice and I viewed this as the crux of the problem.

As I started developing tools to help my teammates enhance their skills, I quickly realized I was not looking for a skill set for customer service. Instead it was a skill set for communication. Realizing that I had not found a system that would provide a framework for practicing these communication skills, I set out to develop my own system for our Cooper Pest staff. The system, What + How = WOW, is not revolutionary, in fact, I borrowed from many different companies. However, it takes several of these concepts and puts them into one neat package which can be practiced, thereby providing anyone who communicates a tool with which to practice.

In late 1997, I launched my first WHAT + HOW seminar at Cooper and we started recording conversations and grading each other. We were implementing the process at Cooper, but I did not realize the strength of the system. Then in 1999, by accident, everything changed.

May 1999 was one of the most important months of my life. It was during this month that I realized the power of WOW and the potential it had within our organization. I also realized how it could help companies all over the country improve the skills of their people when it comes to client relations. At the same time, it can enhance their teamwork.

Gale & Wentworth (now The Gale Company) had developed a concept called service partners in the 1990s. As part of this concept the service partners (vendors of the company) would gather with the senior property managers on an annual basis and being a service partner, I would attend this business meeting as the Cooper Pest Control representative. In May 1999, we were gathered in Amelia Island, Florida for the annual meeting. In attendance at this meeting were Robert "Bob" Palestri, President of the Management Services Department for The Gale Company, approximately 25 Property Managers and 30 Service Partners. The meeting was a chance for everyone to come together in a relaxed setting to help grow the Gale portfolio and to allow vendors to become more familiar with each other.

That year we were staying at the Ritz Carlton and seminars were not part of the mix. Golf and networking events were the order of the day. We had a wonderful group of people and we were having a very enjoyable and relaxing time. On our second day, Bob and his senior team were taking a sunrise—morning walk on the beach and I was invited to come along. As I entered the lobby little did I know that the calm morning would become an opportunity and WOW was about to change forever.

As I entered the lobby, prepared for a refreshing morning walk, I realized there was a problem as Bob was a little perturbed. It turned out that Bob's stomach was upset and he had just left the gift shop in search of antacid. Instead of quickly obtaining the antacid and getting on with the walk, Bob received a dose of inferior customer service and it took five minutes and heartache before Bob found what he was looking for. A poor customer service experience later and Bob was discussing with everyone his inability to acquire the goods he wanted and he was even more taken back because it was inside the Ritz and his expectation was to receive stellar customer service. As we walked on the beach we discussed the pathetic state of customer service and somehow the conversation turned to customer service at Cooper Pest Control.

Walking on the beach, the discussion turned to my WOW process at Cooper. Bob, intrigued by my explanations of how we were implementing this system at my company, wanted to hear more. I was flattered that it actually intrigued him. Up to this point, I did not look at the program as anything more than an internal training tool for my staff. Excited, I told Bob that I actually had my in-house WOW PowerPoint with me on my laptop. No sooner the words were out of my mouth; Bob asked me to give an impromptu seminar at 6 o'clock, that evening to our entire group. There was only one "minor" problem; that was the same time we were scheduled to be poolside, relaxing with a few drinks after a "strenuous" day of golf.

As Bob started speaking to his team about the change in plans for the evening, the laser stares started shooting in my direction from the managers. I was good friends with all of them, but you could see the look of concern and disbelief as the plans for this meeting came together. In vain, I tried to convince Bob that this was not the best idea. After all, and who would want to hear about Cooper's WOW customer service program.

Bob won, and I lost the disagreement. By 6 o'clock, everyone was assembled for an hour long meeting. The room was filled with a group of very unhappy people and for one of the few times in my life, nerves filled my stomach. These were my peers, but I knew the deck was stacked against me.

Little did I realize, but the bases were loaded and I was ready to deliver a grand slam! In the first 15 minutes of the presentation I realized I had more than a just process that worked at Cooper. Everyone was attentive and the room was silent. By the end of the hour I was no longer was being beaten up, but praised for an inspirational talk.

It was then that I learned the power of WHAT + HOW. Discussions followed with my friends over the next two days in Amelia Island as the WOW system took on a whole new meaning to me. Mike Amoroso, the President of Valcourt Building Services of NJ discussed with me the possibility of bringing the program to his team. I had in-depth conversations with others about the benefits of the system and how it could be put to work in a variety of situations. As the days passed the WOW system began to transform from an in-house program into a generic program for any company committed to customer service. Although I have refined it since that memorable day, the framework still remains. It is a system for communication that has changed the cultures of several corporations across the United States.

WOW becomes part of everyday life at Cooper

Recognizing the power of the WOW concept I set about making more changes at Cooper. In 2000, we changed our mission. Previously it was a long mission, which I could not recite from memory. Now it is simple and everyone in the company knows it and understands it:

> ➢ *WOW our clients*
> ➢ *WOW our teammates*
> ➢ *WOW our community*
> ➢ *WOW our service partners*
> ➢ *And WOW the bottom line*

Everything we do at Cooper is to fulfill the mission of WOW. And we use the WOW process to PRACTICE the WOW concepts in order to make this a reality. But it does not end there. WOW permeates throughout the organization. We have WOW lunches every other month where the food we eat must spell out the word WOW. At these meetings we set WOW goals and give out bonuses for achieving them as we strive to fulfill the mission of the company. Once a month we have staff meetings and all members of the company attend. The organization consists of 54 teammates as of November 2003 and we give out WOW dollars to teammates that have WOWed each other. In addition, we give out WOW dollars for anyone who has WOWed an external client. It is really inspiring to see teammates WOWing each other. What I love the most are the messages that our clients leave on my voice mail. Yes, on a regular basis I get voice mails praising our service. There was a time in the not too distant past when the only call I would receive would be regarding a problem or a complaint. Now the voice mails of praise outnumber the complaints 4 to 1. Besides phone calls, I get e-mails, notes on invoices and stories when I am at events with our clients about things the Cooper staff did to WOW them.

Many of these calls and e-mails are a result of a change I made on the work orders we leave with our clients. At the top of each work order is the following paragraph along with our phone number, my extension and my e-mail:

Thank you for your continued support. I would like to take a moment to discuss what we call WOW. It is the embodiment of what we do everyday at Cooper, as you can see in our mission statement on the reverse side of this document. Our definition of WOW is, "WOW is achieved when the experience makes such an excellent impression with the receiving party that it is shared with family and friends. When striving for WOW, the by-product is an incredible experience, which impresses everyone we come in contact with."

Everything we do at Cooper is aimed at WOWing you, our valued client. This begins with every service we render. I hope today's service achieves our WOW standard.

If you had an incredible experience, I would love to hear about it. You can also let me know if we did not achieve WOW. My e-mail and phone number are below. Feel free to drop me a line and let me know how we are stacking up. We want to be the best service provider you hire and this is what our mission is all about.

If you have friends, family or know of businesses that we can WOW, please pass along our name. We would love to add them to the list of customers we WOW everyday.

The team at Cooper thanks you for your continued support.

Phillip Cooper

With the addition of this paragraph to our service orders came an instant recognition within our staff and our clients that WOW was the focus of the organization. Then we backed our words with action. We recognize the need to use the principles of WOW in all of our dealings whether it is with our teammates or the outside world. We are cognizant that we need to apply the same principles to the people that we work with as to the people that we are serving. It is critical that we apply the principles of WHAT + HOW to both our internal and external clients.

Do I get an occasional, "We were not WOWed?" Well, of course I do! And that is when I turn it into my opportunity to really WOW them. Trust me, when I am done conversing with an upset or even irate client they are talking at the dinner table about their WOW customer service experience at Cooper. It is my objective to WOW them and if I fall short I review the conversation with a fine tooth comb.

WOW is a passion at Cooper and it can be your passion, too!!!!!

+ HOW Process

; the system took over two years of
hanging. The system has five steps to
to HOW and 10 overall objectives. Each
aspect of the system could have its own components. I
know I can write books on each particular step and
break them down even further. But in developing the
system, I made every effort to break WOW service into
manageable pieces so it could be easily practiced.

The components of WOW are quite simple. You
must convey the information regarding the subject you
are discussing. Organization knowledge and effective
communication of this knowledge embodies the five
steps of WHAT.

- ➢ *Excellent Product Knowledge*
- ➢ *Communication of expectations*
- ➢ *Clear presentation of the options*
- ➢ *Only communicate what is necessary to make a decision*
- ➢ *Documentation*

The WHAT components are explored in Chapters
three through seven. The WHAT section could comprise
an entire book as this is all about how we train ourselves
and our teammates. I have made the conscious decision
to provide overviews of the WHAT components so you
can implement and use them in the system. Insuring
that you know WHAT you are communicating is critical
in the WOW process. There is so much more to WHAT
knowledge than is contained in this book. I have already
started research for the sequel to this book titled, "In
Search of What" by looking at leading customer service
organizations and how they disseminate information
to their staff for ultimate delivery to the client. The
WHAT section will give you an overview of things to

ponder about from a knowledge perspective in pursuit of the WOW moments.

Chapters nine through seventeen explore HOW you communicate. The 12 HOW steps are unique unto themselves and provide the platform to deliver WOW communication consistently. When developing the steps, I actually came up with 20 unique items, but combined a number of them to keep the number to a manageable 12. 12 simple, but meaningful steps form HOW you communicate:

- ➢ *Exude Confidence*
- ➢ *Customer Friendly*
- ➢ *Smile Factor*
- ➢ *Pace*
- ➢ *Enunciation*
- ➢ *Pronouns*
- ➢ *Names*
- ➢ *Ask Questions*
- ➢ *Listen*
- ➢ *Avoid the Use of Jargon*
- ➢ *Warm and Fuzzies*
- ➢ *Summarize and Conclude*

Soul Mates and Remembering the Steps

Within the HOW Process I have grouped items together, and I affectionately call them Soul Mates. When I think of soul mates I think of a couple happily married for fifty years. Each intricately linked to the other and yet with their own personality. In the HOW process I have grouped six steps together as Soul Mates. Pace and Enunciation, Pronouns and Names, and lastly Ask Questions and Listen.

Looking at each of the 12 steps in concert with the other is critical to the overall process. You can have proper pace, talking at speed that others can understand and keeps their attention, but if you are not enunciating clearly the receiving party simply will not be able to understand what is being said. If you ask questions and then you fail to listen, well, you might as well not have ever asked the questions.

I also use the soul mates as a way helping newcomers to WHAT + HOW to remember the steps. The soul mates consist of three pairs of steps and are sandwiched between steps one through three and steps ten through 12. I think of the HOW steps like an Oreo cookie, the Soul Mates are the creamy middle. The top cookie is made up of the first three HOW steps (Exuding Confidence, Customer Friendly and Smile Factor) the creamy middle is made up of three pairs of soul mates (Pace and Enunciation, Pronouns and Names, and Ask Questions and Listen). The bottom cookie is made up of the final three steps (Avoid the Use of Jargon; Warm and Fuzzies; and Summarize and Conclude).

Three beginning steps plus our three sets of Soul Mates plus our final three steps equals HOW. A nice neat bundle which makes remembering that much easier.

Meeting the Objectives

During my search for excellent customer service I encountered the old adages such as; the customer is always right, make sure you exceed the client's expectations and many other soft items. These are the things that are very hard to practice. Once I developed the WHAT + HOW steps I came back to the essence of customer service. The objectives of WOW are a macro look at the process, and we ask ourselves the questions that ultimately determine if we provided an excellent customer service experience. If we are effective in our WHAT + HOW steps, the objectives simply fall into place. However, it is a good exercise to always evaluate the entire conversation from the pure customer service perspective, which is what these 12 steps do.

The first and last objectives, in the process are the most important.

> ➢ #1 *Did I WOW you (according to the WOW definition)*
> ➢ #10 *Did I build Trust*

WOW experiences and trust keep clients coming back and client retention is the name of the game. We have held focus groups with our clients over the years and the number one reason they choose us is trust. We work very hard at building trust and our "trust quotient" has increased in recent years. I see this in our increased business and client retention. In our industry, 80 percent client retention is considered outstanding. In 2002 our client retention in the residential sector was 93 percent on an annual basis and we expect it to increase even higher. However, each communication we have with our clients affects the "trust quotient" and we need to ask ourselves the questions, "Did we WOW the client?" and "Did we build trust after each conversation?"

The other eight objectives are important, but the first two form the basis for relationship   s   . Once we have formed the basis for the communication we also look at other key objectives.

> ➢ #2 *Did I increase the level of client satisfaction?*
> ➢ #3 *Did I insure the client wants to use our service now and in the future?*
> ➢ #4 *Did I make sure the client perceives value in working with my company?*

> ➤ #5 Do I understand the prospect/client's needs?
> ➤ #6 Did I determine the most appropriate product/service based on our client's needs?
> ➤ #7 Does the client understand his/her options?
> ➤ #8 Does the client know the various products and services we offer?
> ➤ #9 Did I find opportunities to increase value, business opportunities, sales and level of customer satisfaction?

Examining each of the objectives to see if we achieved them allows us to evaluate the success of the communication. If we score high in each of the areas, we are going to achieve the by-product. Remember, WOW moments are rare, but the by-product is what will keep our customers coming back.

Practice Makes Perfect

Baseball, football, gymnastics, opera, the symphony . . . what do they all have in common? Practice. It is one simple word—PRACTICE—that took me down the road of WHAT + HOW = WOW. The Chapter, "Ready, Set, Go. Putting WHAT + HOW into Action," outlines a detailed look at practice and outlines a way to encourage your teammates to practice. And practice is the key to success.

As I watched my customer service team struggle in the late 90s, I realized they were going through classes on what to do, but they were not practicing. In order to practice, you need something to practice and I recognized that we rarely look at the communication process as a series of steps that can be practiced. Creating a system that could be practiced was essential to raising the bar at Cooper Pest Control.

Practice. Athletes, musicians, entertainers all practice their craft. The best of the best practice every day. What makes customer service any different? Nothing. In 1996 I started my search for a method to teach my staff at Cooper Pest Control. I was looking to establish a method they could practice in order to grow into outstanding customer service representatives.

When I think of practice I think of Michael Jordan, perhaps the best basketball player we have seen in our lifetime. As good as Jordan was, he practiced over and over. Why? Because he knew to stay on top of his game, to be the best, he must continue to practice. When Jordan retired from basketball the first time, to try his hand at baseball, his intense basketball practices stopped. When he returned to the basketball court it took him a few weeks to get his game back to his former level.

Practicing everyday, getting his body and mind conditioned for the rigors of the National Basketball Association were essential. Michael Jordan knows what he needs to practice to keep his game at a high level and by practicing and combining it with his natural ability; he performed as the best player in basketball for years.

WOW is no different. Communication is no different. There are so many facets in delivering outstanding customer service that unless they are practiced, delivering that consistent level of service and seizing those WOW moments becomes more difficult.

Can WOW service be delivered without practice? Of course, it can! Can Michael Jordan make a shot, even an important shot, without practicing? Of course, he can! But can he do it consistently and can he create other spectacular moments without practice, I bet Jordan would answer "No!" That is the difference. By practicing and being the best he can be, the moments become his to seize. WOW is the same, practice makes WOW.

Measuring WHAT + HOW,
Record and Grading

Practice is wonderful and practice make perfect. The athlete knows the body mechanics to practice, but what do you practice in the process of communication? As I looked around the country I could not find a system that measured the communication process. It became so apparent when I compared customer services to other disciplines. The professional has a yardstick, some type of measurement to determine their performance level and the customer service representative does not.

How many times do we call places that say the call is being taped for quality assurance? How many of those representatives ever hear their recording? In most cases very few. The tapes are used by supervisors to help in training or in monitoring performance. How many representatives get to hear the recording before a supervisor? Even fewer yet.

The WHAT + HOW system not only provides steps for communication, but provides a system for determining performance levels. By taping conversations and then grading them, the customer service representative goes through a process of self-improvement. I strongly believe the communication process needs to be empowered through our people. They need to recognize that excellent communication is a skill that needs to be practiced and then graded. Grading provides the yardstick from which we can measure our improvement.

The Chapter, *"Ready, Set, Go. Putting WHAT + HOW into Action:"* goes through the grading process which you can implement in your organization. It provides a way to practice and hone our skills. Most of this work is done on the HOW side. What is interesting is that we get better with our WHAT knowledge as others listen to tapes and find holes in our training or process and procedure. It is an excellent quality control tool to help us grow as an organization in addition to providing a method to practice for the customer service representative.

Tapes and the Pulse of the Organization

The Chapter, "Tapes and the Pulse of the Organization" reviews how I am able to use our WOW tapes to gain a pulse on the organization. I have found the tapes invaluable and I will share my experience with you.

Problem Resolution

In every organization there are methods for resolving problems with clients. No matter where I speak, when I ask what the participants would like to gain from the seminar, invariably the number one item is dealing with unhappy clients. The Chapter titled, "Problem Resolution" looks specifically at this topic and ties together a number of concepts from WHAT + HOW to provide a framework for effective problem resolution. I also examine concepts that Commerce Bank utilizes as well as a consultant from St. Louis, June Van Klaveren.

WOW your teammates

WOWing internal and external clients is fundamental to our organizations. The focus of Chapter 22 is on the internal client, our teammates. There are many things we have done within Cooper to bring this point home. I attribute much of our success to the implementation of these WOW programs and they are explored in greater depth in this chapter.

Until recently I thought Cooper Pest Control had the best or close to the best WOW program out there. Then I ran into Commerce Bank. This bank has turned the traditions of banking on its ear and their WOW program is something to marvel. In the chapter "WOW your teammates" I explore the Commerce Bank magic and what they have been able to achieve with their WOW program.

Underestimating the WHAT + HOW process as part of WOW

In preparation for learning the WOW system, it is important to understand how easily it can be misconstrued. My most favorite example revolves around one of my former Cooper Pest Control teammates, Trudy. She fell into the WOW trap of misunderstanding what WHAT + HOW is about. Trudy was new with the company and had been working for one month as an outside commercial sales representative. At that time, we did not send salespeople through WOW training until after the first month. What I observed with Trudy changed all of this. Trudy knew the company's mission and thought she had WOW nailed down. The great part was she was aiming to WOW people, but the problem was she did not understand what we meant by WOW.

One afternoon, Trudy came to me very excited about how she had just prevented a client from canceling our services. Trudy went on to explain the errors we had made with the client and what she did to save them. I was excited for her also, she was brand new with the company and she had stepped up to the plate. Bravo to

Trudy! Saving a client is something to get extraordinarily excited about. I am even certain, based on Trudy's conversation, that the client may have been discussing it at dinner with the family, certainly a WOW moment. Something in my gut was bothering me, but I was not sure what it was. Then I realized that Trudy had never been through WHAT + HOW training at Cooper and now her perception of WOW was simply fulfilling the WOW definition, achieving the WOW moment. Then I started to ask myself questions. Was Trudy achieving the by-product of the definition, was she doing all the things necessary to achieve WOW on a consistent basis. There are five WHAT steps, 12 HOW steps and 10 Overall Objectives that help us find those WOW gems, but how many of those items were being performed successfully, and more importantly, what was the level of consistency?

As I struggled with this, I realized I simply did not have the answer to this question and that is when I changed the way we do business at Cooper. WOW became part of the mantra of Cooper, from our mission, our WOW lunches, WOW dollars, along with the many other WOW moments that support our WOW training. The training is continuous, but starts when our new hires take an Intro to WOW class (1.5 hours) as part of our orientation process and then within four weeks a four-hour class on WHAT + HOW.

WHAT + HOW will give you the tools to find the WOW opportunities and produce the by-product, an incredible experience, which impresses everyone we come in contact with.

Finding Opportunities

Commerce Bank, headquartered in New Jersey makes a point during their orientation of new hires to point out that life is full of opportunities. This point is stressed in everything Commerce Bank does in their sustained effort to achieve WOW.

Finding the opportunities is what makes the difference between the winners and the losers. WHAT + HOW is about helping us find the opportunities that will lead to that WOW moment. There are so many opportunities that we pass by on a daily basis because we do not have our WOW radar on. We are so busy doing our thing that we forget the essentials of the communication process. Are we listening to what the other person is saying to us? Are we taking visual clues from the body language being displayed?. This is just the beginning!

I am sure you have met the person that seems to have everything go right. So often we hear, "Gosh that person is so lucky!" Well, I am a firm believer that people create their own luck. What is different about the lucky people of the world is that they are constantly looking for opportunity and they set the table so the opportunities present themselves.

I have had long conversations with these people and there is one common denominator. They naturally do the WHAT + HOW process. Although they do not consciously think about it, they follow almost all of the steps. They do the things to find the opportunities and then they take advantage of them.

By learning, following and practicing, the steps of WHAT + HOW, you too can create your own luck. Turn your WOW radar on and find those WOW opportunities

CHAPTER 2

The State Of Customer Service Today

"The customer is always right." "We deliver outstanding customer service." "The customer is our first priority." So many companies say they deliver outstanding customer service and yet they fail to deliver.

The bar is so low that mediocre customer service becomes outstanding customer service. The state of customer service in the United States simply stinks. How many times today did you speak with someone who actually practiced the craft of customer service? I doubt very many. How many WOW experiences did you have today? What are you going to speak about at dinner tonight, was it one of those experiences?

As troubled as I am about customer service there are companies that produce the WOW experience. Although they do not practice the steps outlined in this book, the companies and individuals that deliver WOW service have one thing in common, they score consistently high on most of the WOW components. Even though they score high on many of the items, what is striking is rarely do they hit all the marks. Even as good as they are there is still room for improvement; unfortunately the best representatives are not even aware of what they could improve upon. They simply falling into the habits they have learned over the years and some good old fashioned common sense to deliver excellent customer service. With a system to guide them to improvement the best would only get better.

The other issue that I have found in common with most people in customer service is that they really do care about what they are doing. They simply do not understand how to succeed in their profession. So many times we encounter horrible customer service representatives, but I wonder if they even realize what they are doing wrong? Based on conversations with these individuals, they simply are missing the basic skills of effective communication. The result is the appalling customer service we are used to. I view this as tragic that so many people have the desire to WOW, but simply have no idea how to achieve WOW.

What is customer service

Every communication we make is customer service. Whether it is communicating with my children, my wife, my neighbors or business associates, the precepts of customer service are always present. Customer service is about an attitude, a passion for delivering the correct message.

At Cooper Pest Control, customer service extends to my service personnel. If you ask the public what our service technicians or pest management professionals (PMPs) do, they would say they are in the business of killing bugs. How wrong they are. In fact, killing bugs is only 25 percent of a service technician's job. The remaining 75 percent is delivering outstanding customer service, WOW customer service. They can do the best job in the world of killing bugs, but if their customer service skills are lacking, we will not grow and expand.

How about a server at a restaurant? In the chapter of warm and fuzzies you will get to meet Pete from LG's Prime Steakhouse and you will learn why he is the best server I have ever had. On June 19, 2000, Pete scored a 10 across the board on the WOW grading system (1=pathetic, 10=WOW). Yes, a server subscribes to the same WOW methodology and the best servers score consistently high in each of the categories. I wonder about the tips he receives because he is simply super.

Customer service pervades every aspect of our lives. Although this book focuses on the more traditional forms of customer service, these principles can be applied to our everyday communications.

Internal Clients and External Clients

Clients are the lifeblood of any organization. Without clients we would not have products to produce or services to provide. For years, when the world referred to the client, the reference was specifically at what we term the external client, the ones that employ our services and purchase our products/services. This traditional view of the client is undergoing transformation as many organizations have acknowledged there is a second client in the mix, the internal client. The internal clients are the people we work with in our organizations and WOWing them is critical to the success of our respective organizations.

Do we WOW our teammates on a daily basis? Do we even try? What steps does the organization take to instill the belief that WOWing the internal client is just as important as WOWing the external client. For years at Cooper Pest, we simply took this for granted and did nothing special to encourage WOW behavior. In the year 1999, we instituted a number of programs to encourage WOW and we acknowledged the internal client. The transformation of our culture has been remarkable! In four years, we have increased employee retention and increased our traditional growth numbers by 200 percent to 300 percent, while increasing our profit margin.

As I travel around the country, I am surprised at how many people continue to view customer service as dealing with their paid clientele. These organizations go through their daily routine with blinders on. As surprised as I am, I remember that my organization had these blinders on until 1999. Removing the blinders is so very important and a realization that all of the elements discussed in this book are applicable to both the external and internal client.

Even more perplexing phenomena are the organizations that discuss the internal/external client relationship, but when teaching front line customer service or communication, the reference to the internal client ends. While the acknowledgement that the internal client exists, the focus of the organization is directed at the source of direct revenue, the external client.

How messages get confused

How many times do we end a conversation and the wrong message was sent. One of the most enduring comedy skits is the situation where a conversation is misinterpreted and a new set of circumstances are created as the story takes a life of its own. One of the more funny ones was an episode in the 2002 season of NBC's hit show Friends. While I am not an avid fan of television, I catch the show occasionally. I watched this particular episode and was glued to the screen for thirty minutes.

The episode begins with Rachael about to give birth. Ross, who has been trying to decide whether or not to marry her, drops an engagement ring from his pocket next to Rachael's bed without realizing it. Joey comes in, sees the ring and kneels down to pick it up. Rachael looks over and sees Joey on his knee with the ring and is overcome. Rachel says, "Yes" and, Joey, mortified, is at a loss as to what to do next and, unfortunately, does not correct Rachel's error in judgment. For the next 20 minutes, every time Joey tries to correct the situation, he gets interrupted or someone else says something that leads others to believe that Joey has proposed. Toward the end, Rachael finds out that Joey really was not proposing and gets upset with Joey for misleading her. The twist comes when Rachael finally realizes that Joey never popped the question, and realizes to her embarrassment, what happened. WOW.

A funny sitcom or a real look at reality? Misunderstandings like this, maybe not as exaggerated, happen all too often and when it happens in customer service situation the results can be disastrous. It is the responsibility of the customer service representative to insure the client understands the message being delivered.

The Misconception, Excellent Customer Service takes a long time

Can a WOW moment happen in sixty seconds or one minute? If I were to tell you that the WOW by-product of excellent customer service can be delivered in sixty-one seconds, most people would laugh. Could you score high on all marks of the WOW system in 60 seconds? You could and I can prove it.

L.L. Bean has a great reputation for customer service and in 1999 they exemplified that outstanding customer service can be quick and efficient, a sixty second moment. In pursuit of excellent customer service I call a variety of companies around the country and tape the conversations. I am seeking WOW gems or outstanding by-product calls. In 1999, Maureen from L.L. Bean delivered WOW. I still rate it high among my favorites. This conversation is one of the more remarkable calls I have witnessed because, in sixty seconds, Maureen hit all five WHAT marks, 11 of 12 HOW marks and scored high on every objective.

To those critics who claim outstanding customer service takes a long time, I ask them to listen to Maureen who not only provided outstanding customer service, but also did it efficiently in less than a minute.

In a written format, I cannot capture the verbal aspects of the conversation. However, as you read the words that were conveyed, imagine Maureen with a bubbly voice, an enthusiasm for her product, a passion for her job and you have the entire conversation. Here is how the conversation went between Nancy and Maureen.

Maureen: *L.L. Bean, Maureen speaking may I help you?.*

Nancy: *Hi, I was just wondering if you can send me a clothing catalog and also more specifically do you have children's catalogs also.*

Maureen: *Yes, Yes.*

Nancy: *OK, if you could send me one I'd appreciate it.*

Maureen: *Oh, It would give me great joy to do that, I love our kid's catalog.*

Nancy: *Yea, I think the kids look so cute in the outfits.*

Maureen: *Yes. What is your name please?*

Nancy: *First name is Nancy, last name is Kintner, K-I-N-T-N-E-R.*

Maureen: *And your zip code, Mrs. Kintner?*

Nancy: 00000.

Maureen: Thank you. Are you at 2112 Baldwin Court in Yourtown?

Nancy: Yes.

Maureen: Alright, I will send you our kids' spring catalog.

Nancy: OK and also an adult one too, I would like that too.

Maureen: There is a women's catalog coming out in March let me send that one as well.

Nancy: OK, Great.

Maureen: Alright, it takes about 10 days for the catalogs to reach you.

Nancy: That's fine.

Maureen: I will be glad to do that. Well, thanks for calling.

Nancy: Thanks, take care.

Maureen: Bye.

Did Maureen score high on every component of WOW? No. Could Maureen have done better? Yes. But in 60 seconds Maureen captured the essence of WOW customer service. Maureen was sending Nancy her catalogs and Nancy knew how long it would take for them to reach her and had a pleasurable efficient experience. This is the model and standard that L.L. Bean subscribes to and this is why they are one of the premier deliverers of customer service in this country.

Raising the Bar

To achieve WOW customer service we must raise the bar. This is exactly what we do at Cooper Pest Control every day. I see many other organizations raising the bar also. Each of these companies is committed to delivering outstanding customer service to their internal and external clients and they are making substantial investments to do so. Insuring their teams are ready to perform each day is the challenge faced by each company

Delivering outstanding customer service requires a serious commitment on behalf of the organization and everyone needs to be involved. I firmly believe the first step is a realization that customer service is not easy and is much more than common sense. I often call to mind a conversation I had with one of my college buddies, Brian Gruber. Brian is a successful attorney in Washington, D.C. and one day we were discussing the state of customer service. Brian is convinced that most of the mistakes made by people involved in customer service are made from a simple lack of common sense. For more than an hour we discussed the distinction between the elements of WHAT + HOW versus just using common sense.

I see people fall into the trap that Brian is convinced of, but how do you raise the bar on common sense? Granted, common sense is very important, but much more is needed in addition to this. Delivering outstanding customer service is just not that easy. It is not as simple as saying treating our customers like you would want to be treated. There needs to be some type of system, whether it is WHAT + HOW or another, but a defined method of achieving outstanding customer service is as important as maintaining it.

Raising the bar is critical. The companies ranked highest in outstanding customer service continually raise the bar.

Game Day

Game Day—the time when we lace up the shoes and go on the field ready to win the game. All of our hard work, practice, team meetings and all the other things we do to prepare, come together for the defining moment when the score matters.

I believe most organizations fail to appreciate the importance of "Game Day" and many do not even realize game day exists in their organizations. Each and every time we communicate with our clients it is game day. If you attend the symphony, do you expect a dress rehearsal or, worse yet, a practice session? Absolutely not; you are expecting a polished performance; you are expecting game day.

Game day is an awareness that you are ready to deliver your peak performance. Whether we are speaking of athletics, the arts or customer service, being prepared for game day is what matters. We need to show up at game day ready to go, and for the people who are not ready, remember there are many others waiting in the wings to take your place.

WHAT + HOW is about being ready for game day. People involved in customer service, in general, do not understand the significance of game day. Many organizations tape and monitor their calls to insure quality of information. Typically, it is a supervisor doing the listening. I challenge you to find organizations that have the people answering the phones taping themselves, and then listening back to the conversations, in the effort of self-improvement.

Being ready for Game Day takes practice. To practice you need a system and a plan of how to practice. The state of customer service today is mediocre and the reason why is simply because organizations have not made a commitment to be ready for Game Day. Saying "Our customers come first," is simply not enough.

WHAT + HOW is about producing outstanding customer service representatives and getting them ready for Game Day. The next section will guide us through the process of WHAT + HOW, laying out the components that we should practice and be prepared to win every game we play.

CHAPTER 3

What Step I —

Excellent Product Knowledge

Excellent product knowledge forms the backbone of excellent customer service. Without product knowledge our ability to WOW a client is crippled and we will fail to deliver even average customer service. Ultimately, our job is to gain excellent product knowledge and be able to effectively communicate it to our clients.

Understanding the elements of Excellent Product Knowledge could be a book onto itself. A key element in delivering outstanding customer service, is knowing WHAT you are talking about. How many times have you gone someplace and been given misleading or false information by the representative? Worse yet is when you speak to two representatives and they give you conflicting information. When I think of this my mind wanders to an experience my friend Brian had at a major computer retail store. Looking to transfer files from one computer to another, Brian took a trip to this retail giant in search of a cable. He entered the department and asked one of the representatives where he could find the appropriate cable. Instead of getting a simple answer

Brian witnessed conflicting information. Another representative overhead what was being said and joined in the conversation. The two representatives began arguing with each other (in front of Brian) about the best way to transfer the files. One told Brian he needed more software, the other discussed other methods, all Brian wanted was the cable. The argument was so protracted that when I went to visit Brian he could not wait to tell me about it.

When I speak to organizations I always ask a basic question. "Tell me in your organization what product knowledge do you need to have?" Like clockwork, everyone begins listing items that revolve around their product or service. I am surprised at the confused looks when I start describing how the knowledge of the operating software of the company is product knowledge. Our team must have excellent product knowledge. The knowledge they possess includes understanding the process and procedures of the organization, understanding the software they are using, understanding the products or services they are discussing.

I find it amazing how many organizations take it for granted that their staff understands. In the spring of 2003, The Gale Company took a survey of their employees and they asked each of them what was their number one obstacle to success within the company. Overwhelmingly, the answer was internal communication; there was a lack of understanding of the rapidly changing environment within Gale, a lack of product knowledge. Without product knowledge, the steps of WHAT + HOW come to a grinding halt. It is very hard to effectively communicate if you do not know what you are speaking about.

Providing teammates with this crucial element is the challenge we face everyday in business. This is so often the key ingredient that produces successes and failures in business. I could write an entire book on how organizations are providing their team with WHAT knowledge and I am currently visiting companies to learn more about their training and ongoing delivery of WHAT to their teammates.

There are so many methods of delivering this knowledge. Classes, books, on-line testing, on-line classes, one on one training, observation, the list goes on and on. Suffice it to say, this is a huge area. The best organizations realize the learning curve never ends and that consistency is important. Staff in similar positions needs to possess the same knowledge and have access to the same knowledge base. Getting everyone on the same page is the challenge. Let me show you some tools being utilized by other companies to insure the WHAT knowledge of their teammates.

On-line testing and 100 percent

Scoring less than 100 percent is not acceptable. This is the simple rule we use at Cooper Pest Control when evaluating test results for WHAT knowledge.

How would you feel if you call a company and a customer service representative gives you incorrect information? Would it be acceptable to you that during the day that he/she gave 99 customers the correct information, but gave you the wrong information? The answer is simple, at that moment in time, what matters is your information and the other 99 people are irrelevant. In essence, the customer service representative scored 99 percent. WOW, 99 percent is pretty darn good and I would have taken that any day of the week on my exams in college. But, when we are delivering information to our clients, 99 percent is just not good enough. The one person who received the wrong information may have such a bad experience that we get reverse WOW. She will be talking to her family and friends about us, but not in the way we want.

At Cooper Pest Control, the pursuit of excellent product knowledge is a battle we wage everyday. In 2003 we started instituting on-line testing for our staff and I love it. We searched high and low for testing software and we chose one that was first used in the education industry. We purchased our first package in 2000, and recently upgraded to their web-based product and thereby implementing testing for our teammates through the web in order for them to continue the learning process.

What I know to be true is we barrage our staff with e-mails and memos in an attempt to provide them with knowledge, bring them up to date on changes, explain an interpretation of process and more. When striving for WOW, we are exceptionally self-critical and we are constantly tweaking things in the organization. Our ultimate goal at Cooper is to continually provide our staff with updates on information as soon as we receive them. Additionally, we develop questions which are added to our exam question bank. Every time we have an e-mail or memo regarding our product knowledge, we also produce some easy questions that we put into the exam question bank which is then converted into tests our staff can take on-line over and over. The questions we develop are multiple choice in most instances, but sometimes we have list matching. It is wonderful that we have lots of questions and tests, but the key how we use the exams to insure excellent product knowledge.

When our staff takes on-line tests there are two objectives, the score and how quickly the score is achieved. The first goal is to get 100 percent on the exam and the second goal is to increase the speed at which you can score the 100 percent. I believe the questions should not be complicated or too tricky. The objective is for our representative to be able to recall the item quickly when speaking with the client. Scoring 100% with speed is the ultimate goal. Typically, the quicker a person can achieve this on the test, translates to improved recall with the client.

An interesting side benefit of testing in this fashion is that we can find organizational weaknesses. There are many times when teammates across the board have trouble with a test question. This indicates a deeper perplexity within the organization and should prompt action. Remember, life is about opportunities and finding organizational confusion is an opportunity to act before it affects our clients in a big way.

The objective of online testing is to develop WHAT knowledge. The better our teammates are at taking passing the exam, the quicker the information can be delivered to the client. Simply, 100 percent is the only acceptable score when it comes to relaying the information to our client. Inaccurate information is not acceptable.

There are a whole host of options when evaluating online testing solutions. Interestingly, the majority of the packages started in the educational arena. When we first investigated these packages in 2000, I was surprised to see they are aimed at university professors, public school systems and simply the education industry. The emphasis was not on business. Much has changed since 2000 and the testing software industry now views private business as a vast, untapped market. The choices of software and options are continually increasing and will provide you with a host of options.

Purchasing testing software for Cooper Pest Control is one of our best investments ever. The online package we selected, after much research, was LXRÒ. Produced by Applied Measurement Professionals, a leader in licensing and certification exams for professional organizations, LXR is a really clever package that provides an excellent platform to develop tests that help develop excellent product knowledge. We have been using it for three years and are immensely happy with our decision. If you want to learn more about this software, go to their website, http://www.lxr.com.

When we started our research in 2000, we found other packages that were less expensive. I continued to research other packages and found many that were cheaper and others that were more expensive. However, ultimately, I felt LXR provided the best value for the cost (approximately $3,600 when we purchased it) and have never been disappointed

There are many opportunities within every industry to purchase on-line education and testing from a variety of providers. Vendors, trade associations, distributors have all joined in to make available value-added solutions to their clients. I view the in-house test question development and these other tools as two unique areas. One does not supplant the other. With LXR we are able to capture the things that are unique to Cooper, we can capture our culture, our specific product knowledge and the information we wish to convey to our clients, to set us apart from our competition. While this is not offered in industry based packages by combining the two we are able to produce learning tools which assist us in our pursuit of excellent product knowledge. Ultimately, integrating testing into your organization is one way of enhancing product knowledge.

If you consider moving into the online testing arena I recommend that you research the current software offerings, As with all software, new packages are being introduced and older packages are being upgraded. A quick search on the web will reveal the variety of packages currently available in addition to LXR. If you take the leap and purchase testing software there are a few things to consider.

1) *Are you comfortable with the method of classifying questions? This will become important as you have thousands of questions, and they need to be cataloged so you can create effective exams.*
2) *Can you easily group questions together to form new tests?*
3) *Can you track the progress of your team and their test results?*
4) *Can you find questions that many people in the organization are getting wrong?*
5) *Does the software give you the ability to easily jumble the questions on the exam each time the person takes it so they do not remember the order of the questions?*
6) *Does the software automatically jumble the answers to the multiple choice answers so the student does not remember the answer to the question is "A"?*

Remember, if you move forward in this arena, it is an organizational commitment to creating test questions and implementing the tests. However, the end result is better WHAT knowledge and I strongly believe it is a commitment worth making.

Electronic information, Knowledge Bases and Checklists

The age of electronic information is allowing our organizations to be more nimble and to be able to disseminate more information timely and effectively. It is the dissemination of information that is the lifeblood of our organizations.

Kurt Padavano, Chief Operating Officer of Advance Realty Group, a leading real estate organization headquartered in New Jersey, understands the effect that electronic media has had on communicating product knowledge.

As Advance grew from a small, centralized commercial real estate developer into a regional powerhouse with personnel spread across the eastern seaboard, so came challenges of keeping the staff informed. The days of company meetings and memos simply no longer were an effective means of communicating.

Enter e-mail. This has become one of the standards of communication in business. I find it hard to imagine how we operated before the advent of e-mail. It has transformed the ability to effectively communicate change. Padavano views e-mail as the primary factor in Advance's ability to carry messages to their staff. By continually enhancing product knowledge, it helps his team to find those "WOW" opportunities.

There are other tools that can be used to communicate product changes to a staff. A dynamic organization has so much information and changing technology that a customer service representative simply cannot know and remember all of the information. Many companies are utilizing software that accesses knowledge bases. Based on questions and information the representative inputs, knowledge is sent back which is then conveyed to the client. Another really useful tool gaining acceptance is the "Portal concept." Portals are evolving as an Intranet, resource. Intranet is gaining widespread acceptance as more and more companies are using browser based software to enhance the communication within the company.

Internet and intranet are transforming the way we communicate and The Gale Company is taking advantage of the changes in technology. The Gale Company, another successful New Jersey based real estate firm, has successfully deployed a portal in their company. Employees can post information on the portal for everyone to see. When a press release goes out it goes on the portal. If a newsworthy event in the company occurs, it goes on the portal.

Each day when the Internet Browser is opened, the default page is The Gale Company Portal. Throughout their Florham Park, NJ headquarters, plasma screens are placed in each department, constantly conveying information about the company, daily visitors, and much more in an effort to keep everyone informed.

Another avenue of information delivery is what the representative sees when they are actually speaking with the client. We want to provide the CSR with as much information as possible while, at the same time, not overwhelming their senses or their ability to retain the information.

The delivery of information to the representative is critical. The challenge with this technology is how quickly the representative can process the new information.

Afterburner, Inc. is a corporate training company is effectively "deploying" the dissemination of information and ultimately the execution of the information. The Afterburner model; is Plan. Brief. and Execute. Debrief is their philosophy about dealing with our rapidly changing environments. One of my favorite tools they refer to is the quick reference guide. The analogy their team uses is the quick references a fighter pilot has. When something goes wrong in the cockpit there are quick checklists present to jar the memory, especially in crisis situations. The checklist allows the pilot to refocus the memory. Imagine if the team in the cockpit had to pull out a 500-page reference guide on the fighter jet. It does not take much imagination to realize that this would not work. Instead, they have the "checklist" and as Afterburner describes it, there is just enough information to prompt the memory.

We have taken those same principles and applied them to Cooper Pest Control. We have a great reference guide which walks our people through our array of products and services. However, while on the line with a client, it simply is too cumbersome. Memorizing the guide is also not an option. Although we would love to automate the guide and create a knowledge base, this is still in the planning stages. The alternative is a good old-fashioned checklist as prescribed by Afterburner. We have developed a number of excellent checklists, which our representative can quickly use to allow them access to information stored in their human hard drive, the most powerful computer of all, the brain. Combining these checklists with our on-line testing allows us to provide accurate, consistent and concise information to our clients. Are we perfect in our organization? I wish we were. What I can tell you is that we get better everyday and our implementation of these concepts elevates our level of product knowledge along with providing a platform for effectively delivering excellent product knowledge to our clients.

Enhancing Product Knowledge — The Gale Report

Hats off to Stan Gale, Ian Marlow, Carl Seaholm and Trish Theirault at The Gale Company. In his pursuit of excellence, Stan Gale wished to improve the internal communication within his executive team. Concurrently, one of his newest executives, Ian Marlowe was changing the communication style within his operations team. Marlow had recently arrived on the Gale scene, as the

Chief Operating Officer and recognized that his operations team needed to be more cohesive. His team was traveling and 70 percent of the organization was involved in the operations of the company. Marlow asked Trish Theirault and Carl Seaholm took the first crack at designing a new communication system and the product was what would be known as "The Gale Report." The system, which I think is outstanding, begins with a template each manager fills out weekly, describing Wins and Challenges they faced the previous week, goals for Wins and Challenges for the upcoming week along with a few other questions. The information is submitted each Thursday to Theirault who combines the information and then distributes it to the entire operations management team on Monday afternoon.

Stan Gale, founder of the organization and its visionary, saw greater potential in the report and expanded it to his entire executive team, "The Gale Report brings our team together by sharing our successes and continuing challenges each week. With and amongst our Senior Management, it bonds us together and inspires solutions. The knowledge this tool gives us allows our entire organization to feel that they are valued stakeholders," he said.

By taking this operations report and expanding it to the entire management team the chances for WOW increased exponentially. The basic report does contain confidential information, but Gale, Theirault and Marlow saw even greater organizational opportunities. In addition to putting the report together for the management team, Marlow and Theirault pick the top 10 wins and challenges of the week and post them on the company's intra-net portal in a manner that insures the confidentiality within the organization. This provides everyone within Gale to see what management is aiming for during the current week.

"The Gale Report is a representation of all groups, divisions and executive rank within our organization," Marlow says enthusiastically. "With this snapshot and sharing of information, dynamic growth and communication occurs within our organization at an incredible rate. Division to division interaction and responsiveness is not only impressive, but allows all of the moving parts to act as one."

What a great tool for keeping everyone in the loop! By forcing the action weekly, it keeps the organization focused and once again stresses the importance of Excellent Product Knowledge, the lifeblood of our organization. By understanding the wins and challenges of the organization, a world of opportunities is opened up for others. If you do not know what the company is trying to achieve, you can never spot the WOW moment.

Using technology to increase product knowledge — Advance Realty

Kurt Padavano of Advance Realty understands how technology and excellent product knowledge come together. To Padavano, along with providing product knowledge for his team, he is able to increase efficiencies to his company and increase the bottom line. In an article he wrote, "Improving Operating Efficiencies Makes Good Dollars and Sense," Padavano states, "Possibly the most obvious and most convenient way to cut internal costs and manage more efficiently is by utilizing technological infrastructure to its fullest potential. Electronic file management saves abundant time and cuts paper costs. Retrieving specific information is made easier by searching for a relevant term in electronic files, rather than rifling through standard filing cabinets, searching somewhat haphazardly to find the information you need. An electronic purchasing, billing and invoicing system does the same: increases efficiency, improves accuracy and reduces extra paper and mailing costs." I have known Kurt for years and he understands that not only does this provide Advance with operating efficiencies but it provides a wealth of product knowledge to their staff. Educating the Advance team is a priority to Kurt and he knows the value of product knowledge. The technology allows their information to be readily accessible and can be easily conveyed. Hats off to Advance, for staying in the forefront of technology.

What Should you Do?

Take a quick look at your organization and determine how well your people understand the products and services you offer, how well new information is communicated and how well they can communicate all of this to your clients. Look at the tools available such as online testing, e-mail, portals, and reports

When everyone is going towards the same WOW the chances of finding that opportunity increase exponentially. Organizations and people are not lucky; they create their own luck. Excellent Product Knowledge provides the platform for luck. Seek it, get it, and deliver it! You and your organization will be poised for the WOW opportunities and be able to hit that grand slam!

CHAPTER 4

What Step 2—

Communication Of Expectations

WHAT to expect from the delivering party is critical to meeting the objectives of the WOW. When I discuss poor customer service experiences, so many begin with a misunderstanding of what was expected. How many organizations state that their objective is to exceed the client's expectation? The difficulty is so often we have no idea what the client's expectation is.

The Golden Rule of Customer Service

John Manning from Commerce Bank was discussing the Golden Rule as it relates to customer service. We all know the Golden Rule:

> "Do unto others as you would have them
> do unto you."

However, as Manning describes the Golden Rule, it simply does not apply in customer service. Instead we should,
"Don't treat others the way you want to be treated, TREAT THEM THE WAY THEY WANT TO BE TREATED!"

Treating them the way they want to be treated is a simple, but important concept. It is not about how we want to be treated; it ultimately is all about how the client wants to be treated. To achieve the Golden Rule of customer service, we must first understand the client's expectations. Without understanding the client's expectations, we will be striving for an illusionary goal and never find the WOW opportunity.

Understanding Client Expectations

But what are the expectations of the client? Hopefully, through our process we will discover the client's expectations. In addition, to the client's expectations, are the expectations we must communicate regarding our products/services. We must have a clear understanding of both what the client expects and the client must know what to expect from us, without it misunderstandings and UN-WOW moments will occur.

A great example of this would be an example I have in my own organization. We are about to service a client for an ant problem they have had in their kitchen. As part of the process we expect that by the next day there will be a reduction of ants by 25 percent and that over the next two weeks the client should see no more ants. The client calls and schedules the service, but our representative does not communicate the expectation of control. We go to the client's house, deliver the service and, the next morning the client wakes up to find the ants still there. In fact, although the problem has been reduced, actually 50 percent have been controlled, the client calls our office very upset that the ants are still there. Now let's take a look at everyone's expectations. Have we exceeded the client's expectations? We cannot answer this question since expectations were never set.

Has Cooper Pest Control exceeded its own internal expectations? The answer is a resounding yes! We viewed 25 percent control the next day as success and we actually exceeded it and achieved 50 percent. Yet because we did not deliver the expectation during the conversation, we ultimately have failed.

Now, think of the conversation a bit differently. This time our representative communicates effectively and explains that the day following service, there will be a reduction of ants by 25 percent and that over the next two weeks the client should see no more ants. As a result, the client can decide whether this expectation meets their needs. If the expectation falls short, the customer service representative will be aware of it and, perhaps there is a solution and perhaps there is not. What we will avoid is an unknown expectation. At least we have the chance to exceed the expectation of the client which is a wonderful thing.

L.L. Bean

Earlier, I examined a great call with Maureen from L.L. Bean. In addition, to the call being extraordinarily efficient (remember the sixty second call) I love to examine the call from a communication of expectation perspective. As a refresher, during the call Nancy was calling L.L. Bean to order catalogs and by the end of the call Maureen, the L.L. Bean representative had ascertained that Nancy wanted a kid's and women's catalog. Towards the end of the conversation Maureen makes a simple statement and pauses:

Maureen: *Alright, it takes about 10 days for the catalogs to reach you (Pause*
Nancy: *That's fine*
Maureen: *I will be glad to do that, Well, thanks for calling*

What if Nancy needed the catalog in five days? What if Nancy needed it in two days? L.L. Bean understands communication of expectations and by simply stating the when the catalog would arrive on Nancy's doorstep they were able to set the level of expectation. Even more significant is that if Nancy wanted to re-establish a different expectation, she had the opportunity. The two most important items surrounding Nancy's call was receiving the correct catalog and getting the catalog in the time frame she needed it so she could ultimately place an order.

The expectation of delivery of the catalog was such a small item in the conversation and yet it is such a crucial one. By making the statement, "it takes about 10 days for our catalog to reach you" and then pausing, it provided Maureen the opportunity to carefully listen to Nancy's reaction. There may have been verbal cues; we will discuss these in the SMILE FACTOR chapter that Nancy was sending. By pausing after the statement Maureen may have picked up on the cue. I am certain Maureen has other delivery options at her disposal, and by communicating the expectations and listening to the response, Maureen was able to determine if the expectation was acceptable.

I have met many people that try to convince me Maureen should have asked Nancy what type of delivery she would have desired, overnight, two-day, standard or maybe even electronic. I disagree; this may have been too many options and confused the client. The standard of service is regular mail and for most clients that actually works quite well for L.L. Bean. By communicating the expectation they open up the opportunity to explore other options if the standard does not meet the client's expectation. The beauty of the L.L. Bean call is that Nancy ordered her catalogs and understood the expectations in 60 seconds. WOW service can be efficient as it was in this instance.

Communicating the expectation is a must

At Cooper Pest Control, we communicate what to expect after a treatment. We let the client know how long it should take to see results, what results they should expect to see and finally, what steps they should take if the pests still persist. It is critical that these expectations are communicated to the client. By communicating expectations, we avoid a confused or unhappy client. As important as communicating the expectation, we need to be certain the client understands the expectation. There are a number of ways to insure we have delivered the message effectively and we will look closely at this in the chapter on Step 12 of How, Summarize and Conclude.

CHAPTER 5

What Step 3—

Clear Presentation OF The Options

Life is full of options. When you woke up this morning the options were endless. Your first option was whether to wake up or put your head back down. Maybe it was a question of whether to hit the snooze button. Once this hurdle was overcome a choice of sitting up or sliding out of the bed was the next choice. To stretch or not to stretch? Once out of bed, you have to sort through the choices of all the rooms in the house and where you wish to go. While on the way to the rooms, you have to decide whether or not to turn on a light switch? The choices are endless.

Sorting through the options is our first challenge and then concisely presenting the most appropriate options to the clients is our goal. However, to do this we must have Step 1, Excellent Product Knowledge learned perfectly. If we do not understand what the options are, how can we communicate them?

Without excellent product knowledge you cannot see your options

To drive this point home, I love to go back to the waking up example. Pretend for a moment that when you woke up this morning instead of being in the safe confines of your bed that you were in an unknown room. The alarm going off has an unfamiliar tone, and as you go to reach for it, and it is not in its familiar place. The room is dark and you now have to decide what to do next. All kinds of thoughts are swirling in your head. How did I get here? Where are the rooms in the house? How do I turn the lights on? Where is the bathroom? Are there steps in the house? Am I on the first floor or second floor? How many floors does this house have? Could I be in the basement? Just imagine how difficult it is to sort through the options that you have without the product knowledge of the house. Your brain is filled with so much stuff and so many questions that you are on information overload and, at this point, most people cannot effectively process the options, let alone present them to someone else.

Sorting through the options

Assuming we understand the options, we then must sort through the choices and effectively communicate them. It is a challenge representatives are faced with everyday in customer service. How many options should be given to the client in the decision process? We lead busy lives, and when we receive too many options we go on information overload. On the other hand, we like options. Without knowing our options, we cannot make an educated decision. In the chapters on How to Communicate we will look closely at the key to communication, ask questions and listen. I view this as the key to delivering a clear presentation of options. By understanding the client we can pick from our choices and effectively communicate.

The Danger of not understanding options

June 2002 was an exceptionally busy month at Cooper Pest Control. The phone volume was high, and was exceeding the capacity of our staff. When this occurs everyone in the company will pitch in and this including myself. I also love to get on the phones from time to time answering customer service, to keep a pulse on the company. It gives me a chance to record and grade myself as well as practice WOW in a pure customer service setting. When I speak with our clients, I use my first name and avoid using my last name so I get a true read from our clients. I have found, when I say Phil Cooper, and combine it with Cooper Pest Control; customers immediately assume I have a vested interest in the company.

This warm June day would not disappoint me. I received a call from Harriet Marchand. In 2000, she had started a maintenance service with us that included wasps. As she started describing the problem, she explained how disappointed she was with the service since wasps were a continual problem at the house, even after she started the service. My excellent product knowledge bells and whistles started going off in my head. I recognized two problems. First, the service she had purchased in 2000 was a Home Intensive package. As part of this service, if a wasp nest is present we will remove it and treat the area. During our regular visits we look for wasp nests, treat and remove them. In between visits, the client can call us if they see more. But the important factor is that the service does not *prevent* wasps.

Not only were product knowledge whistles going off, but Mrs. Marchand, clearly did not understand the expectations of service. Now I kicked into high gear. I knew we had a program specifically designed to PREVENT wasps from building nests, which Cooper Pest Control calls Wasp Prevention. The question was why was Mrs. Marchand sold a Home Intensive and not a Wasp Prevention?

I started asking a host of questions to see if Mrs. Marchand understood the options which were a Home Intensive program with broad insect coverage including reactive wasp control versus the Wasp Prevention program, specifically aimed at wasps, but without broad insect coverage. As I asked the questions, it became clear the Mrs. Marchand clearly thought the Home Intensive prevented wasps. Worse yet, she did not seem to be aware of the wasp prevention service. We had clearly failed to deliver WOW customer service and, in fact, had delivered below average service. For two years, this client had been paying for a service which could never deliver the expectations she had established. It was impossible to say whether we clearly understood her expectations.

By the end of the conversation, we had turned everything around. We explored the options of the various services she could choose from; we established an appointment to estimate the Wasp Prevention Service for her home and to get rid of the existing nests. In addition, I provided significant credits for the work that had been performed in the past, which had not met her expectations.

Clear Presentation of the Options requires thorough product knowledge, a complete understanding of the product and then the ability to ask questions and listen so the options can be presented. By not doing so creates situations like Mrs. Marchand, where the options are not understood, wrong products or services are purchased and rather than WOWing the client, we develop an unhappy client. In the world of retail or service, there is nothing worse than an unhappy client and between failure to deliver clear expectations and poor presentation of the options, unhappy clients will be strewn everywhere. This can easily be the downfall of an organization and is fundamental to satisfying the client.

Make sure you raise the bar. Insure that you are communicating the options to the client. Do not make the mistake of assuming what the client wants. Ask questions and listen for what the client is saying, reach into your bag of knowledge and clearly present the options to the client. Finally, make sure the client clearly understands the options so an informed decision can be made. By using these steps, you will avoid disappointed and aggravated clients. Remember our objective is to deliver WOW customer service. A clear presentation of the options is a critical component in our quest for WOW.

CHAPTER 6

What Step 4—

Only Communicate What Is Needed

Nothing makes me crazier than when I am trying to make a purchase and the sales associate is showing me things I have no interest in. Only Communicate What is Needed means exactly that, do not over-communicate with the client. There is a very fine line between communicating the proper amount of information and communicating too much. Top sales people learn how to straddle this line during their sales training courses they attend. There are different names for the faux pas such as, spilling the cookies and giving away too much. Each recognizes that new sales representatives make this mistake and sales training teaches the sales representative that once the deal is closed he/she should zipper his/her lip and not introduce new items which could kill the deal.

Some of the same principles a sales person uses at the critical stage of closing can be applied to WHAT you communicate. The challenge is to communicate what the client needs to make the decision, but not say too much. I like to think back to all of the options available to us and the selection of the proper ones. If we were to discuss all of the options with the client, his/her head might explode.

Too many options

Earlier I examined a visit by my buddy to a large computer retailer. A closer look at what occurred helps us understand the damage too many options can deliver. When we left Brian it was a hot summer day in the District of Columbia, and he was looking for a computer cable to do a file transfer from his old computer to his new computer. He had four choices of stores: Best Buy, Office Max, Circuit City and Company X. Brian picks Company X and purchases the cable, but not until he has received more information than he wanted. Hot, bothered and armed with another poor customer service story, Brian will think twice about returning to this large computer retailer.

So what happened to produce this effect? Brian goes into the store, straight for the computer department and finds the cable his is looking for. The sales associate asks Brian if he needs help and Brian makes the mistake of telling him what he is getting the cable for. It turns out that there is a series of methods you can use to transfer the files and the sales associate wanted Brian to be aware of his options. Now, this gets tricky. The client already knows what he wants, but the sales associate recognizes that a mistake might be made. What should the sales associate do? Explain the options or only communicate what is needed to make the decision?.

What would have worked well to make the determination would be questions.

Rep: *"Brian, what type of file transfer are you going to do?"*
Brian: *"I am transferring files from one computer to another using Microsoft XP"*

Rep: *"Are you aware that there can be problems with this type of transfer"*

Brian: *"No"*

Rep: *"Would you be interested in me discussing the problems and the different solutions or would you prefer to buy the cable and try it?"*

At this point, Brian could have said, "I would like to know about the problems," or could have simply said "I am happy with the cable I have picked out." Instead, what occurred, as Brian stood next to the multitude of cables, was much different. There was the initial question about what the purpose of the cable. However, the second and third question never came. Instead Brian received a full dose of techno-jargon about file transfers and what works and does not work. To make matters worse, a second representative standing within earshot did not agree with what the first representative was explaining to Brian and joined the conversation. Now the two representatives were bantering back and forth over what the best solution for Brian's file transfer would be. One wanted Brian to buy a more expensive software solution, and the other wanted him to buy an external floppy drive in case the XP transfer did not work. These were only the choices Brian could remember. Fortunately for this computer store, Brian left with the cable in one hand and yes with another item, an external floppy drive in the other. As things went along, the representative was right. The transfer did not go well with the cable and the external drive did the trick. However, even though the representative was right and saved Brian aggravation and a trip back to the store, the story still stuck in his mind. How we get to the same place in the conversation is extremely important.

In a world where our time is stretched, we need to

know our options, but we don't want communication overload. In many cases we simply do not have the patience or the desire to hear it. In other cases it will confuse us. Sometimes it can even hurt the organization we are working for.

Unnecessary information

Providing unnecessary information can lead to a whole host of problems. It can confuse the client, create organizational issues and simply provide a poor customer service experience. I have a great example where one of our Cooper representatives provided more information than necessary, thankfully not affecting, but potentially creating a disastrous situation for our company.

Andre was new to the organization and was working with our current clients helping to schedule maintenance service visits. When we schedule these visits we attempt to schedule time frames of 8 a.m. to 1 p.m. or 12 p.m. to 5 p.m. However, we recognize that many of our clients have very busy lives, and we can narrow down the time frame from a five-hour window to a two-hour window, 8-10 or 11-1. For those who need an even tighter schedule, we can provide an hour window, as long as the client calls in the day of our visit to find out the time we will arrive. Is this a customer friendly situation? No, but we are always looking to make it more customer friendly and I am certain options abound to make our delivery better. But, this is the method that we have in place for our clients and it works very well for us.

On this day, Andre was speaking with Mrs. Young who scheduled her appointment between 8 and 1. During the conversation Mrs. Young was actually very content with the 8-1 time frame. She was going to be home and had no plans of leaving the house during this time frame. Andre scheduled Mrs. Young and was completing the call when he interjected, "Mrs. Young, we will be at your house on Wednesday between 8 and 1, and if you call in on Wednesday at 8:15 a.m., we can actually tell you within an hour of what time we will be arriving."

From a customer friendly perspective this is wonderful. But let's turn the clock forward to the Wednesday morning. Andre has informed not only Mrs. Young of the wonderful option to call in, but also the other 75 clients he scheduled for the day of the same option. Our three customer service representatives come in at 8 a.m. and get settled in. It is a warm day, and we are expecting busier than normal phone volume as there is an increase in insect activity. Instead of normal traffic as the phones go on at 8:15, there are 50 clients calling between 8:15 and 8:30 looking for their one hour window. Many of these clients are getting busy signals since we do not have enough lines to accommodate this volume of traffic. For the lucky ones who get through, only a few make it to the three representatives who can give them the time frame. The others can leave a message in our voice mail or they could hang up in disgust. Now with 30 messages in the box, and the phone ringing from our normal volume, we are in a no-win situation.

Fortunately for Cooper Pest Control, this scary scenario never transpired. We stopped Andre very early in this process, and he only offered this option a few times. But just imagine the damage that could be done by this over-communication. The client was satisfied with the time frame and had given no verbal cues that it was an issue. And yet, we offered up more information and the results could have had rippling effects.

Must communicate what the company wants you to communicate

Have you ever gone into McDonalds to order a Quarter Pounder and are greeted at the end with "Would you like an apple pie with your meal today?" My answer is always no, and it does make me crazy. Yet, I know the representative had no choice in the question.

There will be times when we must communicate something the client does not ask for. Communicating expectations is an example of one of these items. At Cooper, whether or not it matters to the client, our staff is expected to communicate the control of the pest expectations to the client; that is how many days it will take for our pest management techniques to take effect bring the problem to resolution. By communicating this information, if there is a failure the client knows when to call us so we can insure a timely resolution to their pest problem. Without this information we are setting ourselves up for a customer service failure. With proper expectations comes the opportunity to exceed the client's expectations.

In other organizations there may be mandates from the marketing department to ask a specific question. Only communicating what is necessary to make a decision, does not take away the ability of management to insert additional information into the conversation. However, what must be taken into consideration is the effect this additional information will have—namely it will create confusion in the client's mind.

The line is fine between communicating too much and communicating just the right amount of information. Listen to your conversations. See if you have said too much and adjust your style. Communicating only what is needed to help a customer make a decision will make you more effective, increase your efficiency and will increase your ability to WOW the client.

CHAPTER 7

What Step 5—Documentation

What is documentation?

I view documentation as two separate categories. First, we have collateral, all of the material in writing that exists in our organizations. The second part of documentation is our ability to capture conversations and our ability to review the captured information of others. Both are extremely different and form the backbone of communication.

Collateral

Every organization produces boxes full of collateral material. Brochures, catalogs, fact sheets, promotional material and many other items form the collateral of our companies. The first job is for our teammates to know all of the material that actually exists in the organization. This is a challenge of every organization and is not simple to accomplish. I would like to tell you we have mastered it at Cooper, but we have not. There are still things that our teammates should be familiar with that they are not. Is this acceptable?

Absolutely not! However, rest assured, at Cooper Pest, we work very hard to ensure that our teammates know the collateral material we possess.

By knowing the collateral that exists, you can make it available to clients. This is the key to the collateral. It was created for the clients, and if we do not know it exists, it never makes it into the client's hands.

As I travel around the country, it never surprises me that almost every organization faces this same challenge. By providing our representatives with tools to know what collateral is available; we empower our representatives to utilize the material.

Our websites are another form of collateral. Organizations have learned the power of the internet and how making collateral available to our clients on-line, helps them in their buying decisions. Also, our representatives can direct our clients to our website to obtain the material.

E-mail and attachments are another source of providing collateral to our clients in a quick and easy fashion. The rage of 2002-2003, is the .pdf file and while I am certain, this is the current standard, there will be new opportunities to convey collateral to our clients via other methods in the future.

Intra-net portals are another method of distributing collateral throughout organizations. In small business, portals are still in their infancy, but I strongly believe that they are gaining acceptance and are becoming a way of sharing collateral within organizations. The portal is a means for members of the organization to post information to make it available to everyone on the network. Through technology, the use of collateral and its ultimate delivery to the client takes on new shapes. With these changes come greater opportunities to satisfy the client's needs, thereby reinforcing their satisfaction with our organization.

Why use collateral material

When we are speaking with the client we should always be on the alert for collateral opportunities. If we have collateral on a topic we are discussing, then a simple question should be asked, "Would you like me to forward a brochure (or whatever type of collateral you are discussing) to you regarding the service?" If the answer is yes, and you have choices on how to deliver the collateral such as mail, e-mail, website or other delivery methods, you should provide the client with the choice of delivery.

Collateral reinforces the information we are providing and helps build the trust of our clients. It also reinforces our product knowledge in the client's mind. Collateral can be a powerful tool. Learn what collateral is available to you and then be sure to pass it along to your clients.

The other documentation—Notes

The age of computers and electronic media has enabled most organizations to take their customer service to another level. I commend the organizations that use technology to enhance their level of customer service. Traditionally, customer service reps in call centers did not take detailed notes of the conversations. In smaller organizations, notes have been taken for years as they could be referred back to by one or two individuals. In a call center, the notes would lose importance since so many representatives could handle each call. With the onslaught of client relationship management software, the age of note taking, on a consistent basis has arrived. Taking notes requires skills we did not require representatives to have for years. From the use of headsets, operating software packages that incorporate note taking, to the increased need for better typing skills; the skills of the call center representative are more demanding. In large call centers this is the norm, in small business this concept is slowly catching on. However, organizations that have their staff take notes, significantly increases the WHAT knowledge of the organization and enhances the flow of communication.

The ability to document calls in a quick and efficient manner begins with software. Can a customer service organization do it without software? I suppose it can, but in my travels, note taking has been missing in call centers without electronic note taking ability. Long before the computer age, sales representatives were voracious note takers, but this was because they were taking notes for themselves or a small team of sales representatives. But the communication of notes between large numbers of teammates was not possible until client relationship management software was developed. With the advent of client relationship software comes the ability to transmit large amounts of information throughout the organization to further enhance customer service.

There are so many quality packages available today. Some are specifically created for client relationship management; others are industry specific. What is common with the quality packages is the recognition of the importance of note taking. The better packages recognize there is more to the process than just the ability to take notes. How the software flows with the phone call is truly the key. If the software does not make it easy to facilitate note taking while doing other customer related functions, the chance for quality notes decrease.

The ease of taking notes and quickly bringing them back up for review will either make or break the process. If the process is difficult, then HOW we communicate will suffer as we struggle to get the notes into the system while trying to listen to the client and complete other functions of the software. When you combine a simple note taking process with headsets and excellent typing skills, the stage is set for excellent documentation.

American Express

The importance of note taking is apparent at American Express (Amex). Every conversation is meticulously recorded so the next representative has a record of what has occurred. Try calling American Express sometime, then end the conversation and call back a minute later. What you will find is consistent, outstanding note taking on the part of the call center representatives at American Express. Another interesting facet of AMEX is their ability to utilize notes at the beginning of the call. Sometime in 2002, I noticed a change in the way they began their calls. The representative begins the call by asking for your name and permission to review your notes, which they advise will take approximately two minutes. What is interesting is it almost never takes two minutes for the note review. I often wonder if anyone ever tells them that they cannot review the notes. The bottom line is the representative gets a chance to see the most recent conversation and is poised with knowledge about the client. Compare this to a situation where you are on the phone with a representative for 15 minutes and you get disconnected or simply run out of time. Unfortunately, this organization does not take notes, and when you call back, you have to start over from square one. At American Express this scenario will never happen. It is one of their commitments in their quest to provide excellent customer service.

Notes and Small Business, Marathon Data

Client relationship software is quickly making its way into small business and into software packages. From internet-based packages such as Salesforce.com to industry packages, i.e. Marathon Data's PestPac.Net, there are affordable options available to small businesses looking to take the next step in customer service. In the pest management industry, the state of software conducive to successful client management had been lacking. That was before Marathon Data burst onto the scene with its .Net software in 2001. Designed for the service industry, this package allowed my company to enter the big leagues when it came to note taking. Although, originally designed for the pest control industry, this software is applicable to any service based industry and notes are only a part of its overall customer service appeal.

What impresses me about this software is that Marathon uses it to drive its own client management services. All of their representatives use it everyday as part of their interaction with the Marathon client base. Marathon also recognizes the importance of notes, and just like American Express, you can speak to anyone of their representatives and notes are present from the previous conversations. In addition, to a major commitment to producing an outstanding software package, Marathon's President, Mike Ayars, has made the ultimate commitment to deliver quality customer service, what Marathon terms "customer support" to its clientele. Note taking is a prerequisite at Marathon and their staff only knows one way to take notes and that is with quality.

Ayars has also taken note taking to another level. Recognizing the importance of the quality of the notes, each team leader in the customer support group begins his or her day by reviewing the notes of the previous day. A quick glance gives a recap of the customers who have called in, the problems they were having, and just as importantly the quality of notes the representatives are taking. This is especially important as new representatives are hired. Walk into Marathon's headquarters in Oakhurst, NJ, and you will find a small business armed with a big business toolkit, headsets, quality client relationship software and a group of representatives ready to WOW their customers. First class customer service is possible and does happen. It just takes a commitment and desire to achieve. Marathon and American Express do it and so can you!

CHAPTER 8

Overview of HOW

Excellent WHAT knowledge provides us the ability to see those golden moments, those WOW opportunities. HOW is different. HOW we communicate the WHAT knowledge becomes the backbone of WOW. You can be the most brilliant person in the world, but if you cannot communicate your thoughts effectively, WOW will never be achieved.

During 1997, I struggled at Cooper looking at our customer service. As WOW evolved over the next two years, it was the HOW portion that I kept coming developing and changing. In all of the books I have read and all of the seminars I have attended, no one broke the HOW portion into meaningful chunks.

When I started breaking the process down, I recognized there are many key ingredients to HOW and each is very different. As I have grown with the process, I have also recognized that I could take the 12 steps and easily turn them into 20 steps. I have resisted adding more than 12 steps to the process in order to maintain a manageable system for the person practicing HOW. As a result, in some of the steps you will find multiple facets which could be steps onto themselves.

HOW begins with three unique components: Exuding Confidence, Customer Friendly and the Smile factor. It then has what I affectionately call three "Soul Mates:" Pace and Enunciation, Pronouns and Names, Ask Questions and Listen. We finish with Avoiding the Use of Jargon, Warm and Fuzzies and the final step Summarize and Conclude.

There are twelve key ingredients to the execution of WOW. Practicing these key ingredients is the key and the best representatives will take this portion with them where-ever they go. Once you have the ability to score high HOW marks you are in a position to excel in any customer service position. Once you learn the company's WHAT knowledge you will be spotting those WOW opportunities. By learning HOW to communicate, you will be poised to be the best you can be. All that is needed is to know HOW we communicate and the methods of practicing the craft of HOW. So HOW do we do it?

CHAPTER 9

HOW Step 1—Exude Confidence

When I think of exuding confidence, I picture confidence oozing out of the pores in my skin and I picture it as rays of light streaming out. There is so much confidence in me, the magical rays of light, it just keeps beaming or "exuding" out. The confidence beaming out of my body is such a vivid picture and it is how I envision exuding confidence.

Exuding confidence happens when you have a command of the entire WOW process. The result will be the receiving party saying to themselves, "WOW, that customer service representative knows what they are talking about!"

So often we will find ourselves in difficult situations. We begin to struggle with our WHAT knowledge and we are very unsure of what to say next. We may even trip over our words. When we do this the other HOW steps suffer. All of this will come out in other parts of HOW. But the net effect is that we are not Exuding Confidence. The minute this happens we will lose the trust of the client. If they are not confident in our ability to do our job, then how will they ever trust that what we are doing is correct?

There are many things that will exude confidence and just as many that will not exude confidence.

Let's first pick on the things that will hurt us in having confidence oozing from our pores.

Case of the Ums

Ums are a habit many of us have and they are a tough habit to break, "I can get someone out to you in one hour, UM, would you like me to schedule this for you?"

UM is a killer term. It is the term that infers the mind is thinking of what is coming next. In public speaking one of the first things you learn is to avoid the use of UM. Pausing and having a second of silence is far better than UM.

We must be very careful not to use this term when conversing with clients. If we have a command of the process and it is flowing then we will not hesitate and use UM. We are indicating our hesitation, when we use the term, which does not bolster the confidence of the receiving party. We actually can have command of the entire process and be in a position to exude confidence, but if the um word creeps into the conversation our credibility is compromised.

Sticky Black Tar

Interestingly, a customer service representative can exude confidence in the wrong direction and infuriate the client. I term this "black tar." Instead of the positive rays of light coming out of my pores I picture myself stepping into blacktop sealant on a hot sunny day and the sticky tar is stuck to my shoes. The situation in customer service that creates black tar surrounds the confidence that customer service representatives display about policies and procedures that produce

Un-WOW moments. It is the situation where you cannot get the answer you want and the representative confidently tells you the reason is the "policy say" or "our procedure is." One of these moments happened to me when I was out with my friends and the memory is etched in my memory forever.

Going out for an evening with my wife and friends can turn into an adventure. I do not go looking for trouble. I even tone down my customer service expectations so we can have an enjoyable time. However, my friends know that if we run into a really poor experience it is hard for me to sit back and do nothing. Saturday April 15, 2000 happened to be one those evenings. My wife and two other couples, Todd and Linda Baker and Patrick and Diane Rosenlieb, were going out for a relaxing evening after a long week.

It was around 10:15 p.m. and we decided to grab some drinks and appetizers. We picked a restaurant / bar that we had seen, but not been to, the Soft Shell Café. Now the Soft Shell is in a mall right next to the AMC movie theater. Recently the mall had undergone major renovation and this new restaurant had opened. We were hungry and not looking to have a late evening and this restaurant seemed like a good choice. As we approached the restaurant our spirits lifted further and we knew it was going to work out as, the bar was half empty and there were approximately 10 tables inside not being used.

We went inside and sat down at a round table right across from the bar. We waited for a server to come by and after about five minutes we started to scratch our heads wondering why we were being ignored. I went to the bar, ordered drinks and sat back down. Shortly after getting our drinks the hostess came over and informed us that we needed to get up since this was for restaurant seating only.

The oozing of confidence started. But instead of good rays of light there my feet were stuck in black tar. You can exude confidence, but in the wrong direction. The hostess seemed annoyed that we had sat ourselves down in an area that was "off-limits." It was her job to assign the patrons to their appointed seats in the restaurant and we infringed on this responsibility. So it was with attitude that we were dismissed from our seats.

We were confused since so many tables were empty, but we got up and went back to the hostess area and prepared to go through the correct process. I was still very calm and was poised to let things go since creating a scene was not going to make the evening relaxing. As we stood in the hostess area, the hostess started exuding more confidence. She asked if we wanted smoking or non-smoking as if we had just arrived. I replied that we preferred non-smoking.

What came next was astounding. She informed us there was a 20 minute wait to be seated as they were short staffed. I explained we actually did not need to be served, and that we would be more than happy to go to the bar and place our orders there. I also asked if we could sit where we started, which I felt was somewhat reasonable, since only seven tables were filled and approximately 23 remained empty.

Our hostess then provided an explanation of why this was impossible. The hostess explained the restaurant had a rule about cleaning tables and unless the table is cleaned first, patrons are not allowed to be seated. All the tables in the bar were included in the cleaning policy and we could not seat ourselves. More black tar, and it was getting stickier, as she confidently enforced her corporate policy, which made no sense.

Up until this point I had contained myself and gave her room to find a solution. I suspect she thought telling me the rules would be sufficient, however it was not. Now she became annoyed with me. Furthermore, when I am the client and someone gives me attitude, well that is a bad thing. My friends started jostling me to just leave, and let it go. Being a stickler for WOW, I could not. Quickly, my friends distanced themselves from the scene of the crime, and I could hear my wife, Laura cringing and explaining to them what was yet to come.

I asked to speak with a manager and was quickly shot down. Confidently, exuding black tar, she informed me that was not possible. Now it was a battle of wills, and she forgot I was the customer. More black tar. Her confidence stemmed from her knowledge of their rules and the lecture began about their policies and procedures.

I found it very hard to believe that a manager was not available. How could a three-quarter empty restaurant with an angry patron not have a manager available? Stop and think about the situation. We wanted to sit down, have drinks, and possibly order appetizers. With over 10 tables available in the bar, we were told that was not possible. On top of it, I was denied the opportunity to speak with a manager. Definitely not WOW and I certainly did not trust them.

Totally befuddled at this point, I retraced my steps and asked why we could not go back to where we were seated. The hostess said that was a smoking area and that we had requested non-smoking. Our preference was non-smoking, but our original location was fine since no one was seated anywhere in sight anyway.

It baffled me that she never bothered to try to clarify if where we were seated was OK after our non-smoking request.

With this new knowledge, I asked if we could go back to our original seats, but was rebuked. The wait would be five minutes as she explained, the corporate policy was, "no one could be seated until the table is cleaned and set." In fact, the table we were originally at, now working on 15 minutes was fine with us and was clean to our satisfaction. The hostess refused to seat us and again said it was against policy for us to be seated until the table was clean.

Her confidence in her ability to battle me was building. But the confidence in establishing outstanding customer service was going down in flames.

With that I decided the battle was simply not worth the wait I was creating for my wife and our friends. So, I decided to end the battle and instead send a letter to the manager of the restaurant. "Can I please have the name of the manager on duty," was my question.

You can only guess what happened next, of course, more rules and regulations. Exuding the wrong kind of confidence, the hostess informed me that she was not permitted to give out this information and she walked away, oozing more of her brand of confidence.

As I started to leave, a new face appeared. The person introduced himself as the assistant manager and asked if he could help. I informed him that it was too late for help; I changed my request, and asked for the name of the corporate president and mailing address. The hostess snickered at this request, but the assistant manager asked her to provide it to me. I had to wait another four minutes to get the address, but was not given the name I requested. Instead, I was informed I had to call the corporate office to get the remainder of the information. In addition, they would not supply me with the telephone number.

During all of this, the hostess and the assistant manager kept repeating the corporate policy of having to set the table before we could sit.

As frustrated as I was, I really felt terrible for the hostess and the situation she was put in. This is not unusual in the world of customer service and it begins with how management conducts itself and the energy they put into providing a WOW experience. The hostess was either a high school or college student, and was trying to do her job. My anger and frustration were aimed at management who had empowered her to exude this bad confidence; black sticky tar.

WOW is all I can say! The restaurant remained open for two more years after this incident, but they were never packed in spite of their prime location. In mid-2003 the Soft Shell Café closed its doors. During the two years the restaurant remained open after the incident, I never went back, but whenever I passed by I looked, out of curiosity, to see how crowed they were. Always empty and it did not surprise me. I did write to the President and he called me to discuss the letter and we had a lengthy conversation. He candidly told me they had problems which he was going to resolve. He also offered me the opportunity to visit the restaurant, and give him an update on how they had improved. Dinner would be on the Soft Shell. Well, not surprisingly, the certificate never arrived, I bet they did not raise their level of customer service at the restaurant and now the place is boarded up. Black sticky tar is a bad thing.

Do not hide behind policy and procedure

The Soft Shell story is an example of how we can hide behind policy and procedure of our company to create a really poor customer service experience. What infuriates me is when company representatives hide behind the policies and procedures of a company in the process of working with clients. Phrases like, "It is our policy" "Our procedure requires us to . . . ," should be eliminated. I am sure that if you search your memory over the last month you probably can find at least one instance where you were the client and heard these phrases. There is nothing more aggravating than to hear these words. I really am not interested in what the company's policies are. I am not interested in what the company cannot do for me; rather I want to know what they can do for me. I am the client, although I do not need to be catered to, I do expect quality service.

Whenever I discuss Exuding Confidence, I am clear that we should never hide behind policy and procedure. When we hide, the black sticky tar starts getting stuck to our shoes. I teach all of my clients the worst thing they can say is "It is our policy" or "Our procedures require us to . . ." It is very important to avoid these phrases at all costs. Find some other way of positioning the situation. Of course, there are times when you cannot do what you would like when working with a client. We have to work within the rules of our company, but it is the job of the customer service representative to exude positive confidence about the choices available, instead of hiding behind the options that are not available. Never stand behind policies and procedures; they will begin oozing out of you creating something far less than a WOW experience.

How to tell if we are exuding confidence

Determining whether we are exuding the right kind of confidence is quite simple. All you have to do is listen to the client. It is really that simple yet difficult. How the client responds to your communication will determine if you are exuding confidence and if it is rays of light or black sticky tar.

Listening to a recording of the conversation makes this much simpler. By concentrating on the client's reaction, we can determine if we exuded confidence in the communication. Some of the key questions are: Is the client getting annoyed and does the client sound confused or do they hesitate when we speak to them?

I love listening to tapes where the receiving party is the recipient of exuding confidence. You can hear it in their confident responses to the questions they are asked. You can hear it in how the call ends. When confidence is flowing, trust is built and there is no doubt about it.

Annoyed clients

I thoroughly enjoy the opportunity when a client begins the conversation annoyed. Of course, I am not happy that they reached the point of getting annoyed; in fact this really is unacceptable. Most of the time an annoyed client is upset before they ever get to me, which is why they have requested to speak with me. Unlike the Softshell Café, Cooper Pest Control employees are trained to win back the favor of the client. If the client requests to speak to the owner then it is the owner they get. Once I take the call and I hear the concern in their voice, I view it as a personal challenge for to me to regain control of the conversation. What I do when things go wrong separates WOW customer service from mediocre customer service. If I am exuding positive confidence and have a command of the WOW process then it sets the stage for my ability to turn a bad situation into a WOW moment!

Exuding confidence is key when working with frustrated clients. Remember, exuding confidence means we have mastered the other 11 steps of HOW along with the WHAT knowledge. It is the challenge of putting it all together, exuding confidence to turn it around; and when I am successful there is no greater feeling. In fact, these are some of the best opportunities to deliver that WOW moment—a moment that the client will discuss at dinner. Taking that annoyed client and exuding the proper confidence can be a defining moment.

Mastering the system will allow us to have confidence in our method of communication and, providing the client with the WHAT knowledge we possess will enable us to exude confidence. Exuding confidence only comes when we are in control of the system and that is what WOW is about.

CHAPTER 10

HOW Step 2—Customer Friendly

Why can't customer service be like talking to a neighbor, that is, a friendly neighbor? I often wonder this after a poor customer service experience. What I am trying to achieve, is simply a nice friendly conversation; it should just flow. Imagine trying to provide excellent customer service while yelling at the client? Or, take it to the other extreme. Imagine listening to someone who is talking so softly that you get lulled to sleep.

I find the discussion of customer friendly an area many customer service gurus focus on. It is the subject of book after book, seminar after seminar. The experts examine items that make clients feel good and discuss the things we should avoid that annoy the client I agree with the experts on the importance of a customer friendly experience and its importance is exemplified as step two in the HOW components.

Of all of the steps in WOW, Customer Friendly has the greatest single impact on the overall experience of the client. Although Customer Friendly is only one of fifteen steps in delivering the WOW moment Customer Friendly, can in one foul swoop, make or break the process. Many organizations work exceptionally hard on providing that customer friendly experience and I commend them for their commitment. Being customer friendly forms the basis for customer service. Without customer friendly we are left with nothing, but a shallow effort to the client.

When looking at Customer Friendly there are three areas that I believe are critical in succeeding in a customer friendly process.

> *Conversational Tone*
> *Understanding and Avoiding Unfriendlies*
> *Delivering Friendlies*

Conversation tone begins with talking to our client as we talk to our friends and neighbors (that is, a friendly neighbor). Having a friendly conversation with our clients is a simple, but effective tool which we will explore. Understanding and avoiding what I term as unfriendlies is critical in the process. Unfriendlies are the things that just simply annoy us. In fact, when I was searching for a customer service model I found the unfriendlies focused on over and over again. I could write an entire book about unfriendlies and many books have been written about this subject. Finally, finding the Friendlies, the things that make the client feel great will enable us to deliver those WOW moments!

Customer Friendly is about setting the table for the WOW opportunities and without question it is the most critical single item in the WOW process.

Conversational Tone

How many times have we been called to place an order over the phone, trying to get technical help, scheduling a service for our air conditioner and the representative on the other end of the phone is simply not pleasant. How many service people come to our residence and their demeanor is less than stellar? What we are searching for is the customer friendly aspect of How to Communicate. Is it too much to ask that the person treat us in a friendly manner? I subscribe to the notion that this is a basic of customer service. If you treat someone friendly fashion it will go a long way in setting the stage for other good things to come. It really is as simple as pretending we are having a nice neighborly conversation.

When we are with friends, we are relaxed in our conversation and that is the atmosphere we are trying to create in our customer service conversations. The communication needs to remain professional, but at the same time it can be relaxed. Everyday, I encounter people that just do not understand this concept. They are curt, nasty, abrupt; anything, but neighborly. I often wonder if this is how they treat their neighbors, and I am certain many of them probably do go home and are just as unfriendly. This type of attitude has no place in the world of customer service. It is simply unacceptable.

Another trap representatives fall into is saying things that simply are not conversational in nature. In 1999, we called Gateway to check on an order and we had our tape rolling. The representative obviously had heard it was important to say the client's name, but this time it was taken to the extreme. My assistant, Nancy called Gateway and over the next two minutes the representative said Nancy's name eight times. Yes, eight times!!!! Try talking to your friend and say their name eight times in a two minute span and see if it sounds forced or contrived. From my perspective, it sounded ridiculous and it was certainly not conversational.

Professionals who serve customers know that everyday they must persevere through whatever their trials and tribulations are to deliver that consistent pleasant conversational, neighborly tone. When we are not feeling well and when we are stressed this is one of the first things to suffer with most representatives. Taping, which we will discuss in detail in later chapters, the conversation on a day when we are not at our best will give us tremendous insight as to how customer friendly we can be when we are at our worst.

The conversational tone includes so many aspects of HOW as they all get melded into what I consider customer friendly. The Smile Factor, Pace, Pronouns, Names, Listening, Warm and Fuzzies are the specific HOW steps that all enter into the Customer Friendly realm. The conversational tone takes all of these into account as we strive to be as neighborly as possible.

Unfriendlies

The world of customer service is full of unfriendly experiences. We call a company and get stuck in their automated attendant and as hard as we try, we cannot figure out the correct sequence of entries to get to the answer we need. Worse yet, we cannot find a method of speaking to a live human being. Another day we call and the phone rings and rings. Finally after 10 rings someone picks up and quickly puts us on hold where we wait for 15 minutes. Unfriendlies abound in customer service and they are customer service killers. Let's explore a few in depth.

Unauthorized hold

How many times have you placed a phone call to hear, "Thank you for calling ABC Company please hold." CLICK. The next thing you hear is music on hold or worse, dead silence. I call this the unauthorized hold.

Were you ever asked if it was OK to be on hold? The answer is no.

Unauthorized hold sets the tone for the conversation and makes it an uphill battle for whoever will eventually speak with you. If the company has to put you on hold, at the very minimum, you should be asked if it is acceptable and hopefully, you will say yes.

So what happens if we call a company and they ask us if it is acceptable and we say no? It is quite simple; another unfriendly is likely to happen. In most instances the reason we are asked to hold is because there are other people who are waiting in queue or other phone lines are ringing.

It is easy to say we should have more help on the phones, or have better call distribution. However, there will be situations in all organizations where the call volume outstrips the capabilities of the available staff. It is simply a reality. The better organizations reduce the frequency and make it a rare occurrence.

Incessant Rings

When we are on a phone call, the first impression is not the voice you hear answering the phone. What comes first is the number of rings it takes to answer the phone.

How often have you placed a call only to have the line ring numerous times until it is finally answered? A company can have the best customer service in the world, but it is behind the eight ball before it even gets started if the phone is not answered quickly. First impressions are important since you never have a second chance to make that first impression. The number of rings makes the difference. The opposite of incessant rings is what I term, "the two-ring" answer.

Later in this chapter, when I look at what is customer friendly, the two-ring answer is explored further.

Can you please hold while I find out

In our organization, we stress never to give out information, if you are unsure of the correct response. It is better to let the client know you are not sure, but will find out the answer. In the same breath it is important to not keep putting someone on hold while the information is being obtained. Simply put, a lack of WHAT knowledge will translate into an unfriendly phone call.

Another problem also comes to light in this process. These types of calls are not generally morale boosters with the customers. If I have to ask the client to hold more than once, it sends the message I do not know what I am talking about which in turn will erode away at my own confidence. I view not knowing an answer to a question and the lack of WHAT knowledge as two very different things.

It is imperative that we give our representatives the tools that they need to provide the friendly experience our clients deserve.

Lengthy hold times

Waiting on hold for lengthy periods will drive almost every client crazy. As I travel around the country and I ask about things that are "unfriendly in customer service," lengthy hold times are in the top five responses and we can certainly relate since it has happened to all of us.

I have a great example of a company that prides itself on customer service making the fatal mistake of putting someone on hold for what seems like an eternity.

I had one of my staff members, Nancy call a major retailer to find out about shoes. This company which we all know, is one of the leaders in customer service in the country, and is noted for their commitment to the client. However, on this day, they did not shine; even the greatest can have a bad day.

Nancy placed the call, looking for size 5 blue pumps. Paula answered the phone and it was immediately apparent she knew her shoes and the stock available in her department. She had excellent product knowledge and was intent on finding out if the shoes Nancy was looking for were available. After about two minutes of discussion with Nancy, Paula made the decision she needed to take a run into the stock room. Paula asked Nancy if she would mind waiting for a minute while she checked to see if there were any other shoes in stock.

What happened next shocked me—to me it is inconsistent with the retailer's model of outstanding customer service. Paula put Nancy on hold and there was dead air. This store did not have any music-on-hold. I would have preferred music, but it was not Paula's fault that they did not have it. The key ingredient is that Paula asked Nancy if she could hold for one minute. Instead what Nancy received was two minutes of dead air time. Not acceptable. Under the circumstances at least Paula could have asked Nancy if she wanted to wait the couple of minutes or would like a callback. Perhaps she could have told her that there would be dead air while she was gone. But remember she asked Nancy if she could hold for a "minute" and my definition of a minute is 60 seconds not 120 seconds. Although a two-minute hold-time is really not all that bad and actually probably was acceptable while Paula went to the stockroom, the way Paula handled it set the stage for an unfriendly.

How many times do we call a store or a customer support center only to be left on hold forever? In the Northeast we have a service called EZ-Pass which allows us to electronically pass through toll plazas on the roadways. The EZ-Pass staff has my record for lengthy hold times. Recently, I was driving through the toll and a message appeared, "Please call EZ-Pass." Obviously something was wrong with my transponder. So, with my cell phone on and my trusty headset on, I called EZ-Pass to learn what the problem was. The automated attendant came on telling me that they were experiencing high call volume and that someone would be with me shortly. Five minutes passed then ten. I started to wonder if I should call from home since I was on my cell. My customer service curiosity would not let me hang up. Fifteen minutes turned into thirty minutes. Now I was wondering if they would ever pick up.

As I sat waiting for someone to help me, I wondered why this was happening. Was the issue that they could not hire enough representatives to field the calls; or, was the problem that their staffing decisions created a situation where lengthy hold times were expected. I concluded that no matter the reason my hold time was so long, this was probably not an unusual occurrence for clients calling EZ Pass.

My mind then switched to how other companies deal with excessive volume into their call centers and what could EZ Pass do to offset this horrible experience. It is common these days to reach call centers that have automation in place that tracks inbound volume, the number of customer service representatives that are "logged into the systems" and calculates the wait time for the next available representative. The automation then advises you how long until the next representative will be available. Although I do not find this the best customer service practice, at least I can make a rational decision on whether to hold or call back. At

EZ-Pass, this technology did not exist the day I called. They only had a recording thanking me for holding. I cannot remember if there was music on hold or information on hold, but I remember the wait extended to 45 minutes. Finally at minute 52, a representative answered the phone. Not only was I frustrated by the intolerable hold time, I was then greeted with a representative who was not customer friendly.

About three weeks later my misery with EZ-Pass was replicated but this time, the experience was much worse. Fortunately for me, I was the witness and not the recipient. My brother, Rick, was calling EZ Pass to correct issues with five vehicles using the EZ Pass unit. My 52 minute experience was small potatoes compared to the 2.5 hour ordeal my brother dealt with which included multiple lengthy hold times and his call being transferred from one representative to another. I have heard EZ Pass has made great strides in their effort to improve their customer service system. Always better late than never.

New Hires and Frequent Hold

When we hire new staff members at Cooper Pest Control, I am always reminding our staff to insure that our clients are not to suffer while the new representative is learning the ropes. We work very hard to insure before we put a new person on the phone that they have excellent product knowledge. However, there will be occasions when a question is asked that the representative does not have the answer. How the representative handles these challenges becomes critical in insuring a friendly experience.

A common occurrence for new hires in this situation is to ask the client to hold while they obtain an answer to the question. I am fine with this, but where I draw the line is when I am put on hold more than once. Each successive hold on the same call increases my dissatisfaction with the customer friendly aspects of the call. The client should not suffer when a representative is researching answers. Rather than putting the client on hold the customer service representative should provide options to the client. Some of the options include:

➢ *Transferring the call to a representative who has the answers.*
➢ *Offering the client a call back (be sure to let them know when the return call will occur) from someone in the organization qualified to answer the question(s).*

Talking in the Background

I am amazed at how often I will be shopping in a retail store and the staff members of the store are speaking negatively about their workplace. Just as bad is when I am on the phone and I hear foul language in the background. Talk about unprofessional! Both situations are as unfriendly as it gets and results in lost dollars as clients are turned off. Talking in the background occurs all too often and is a customer service faux pas. This is a major unfriendly.

Chewing Gum

Chewing gum is another unfriendly that should not occur. When I go to the counter to purchase an item I do not want the cashier to be chomping away on a wad of gum. Gum chewing affects our ability to enunciate clearly and can be a serious distraction during the communication process.

Commerce Bank takes gum chewing seriously. They view chewing gum as a "no-no" of customer service and I applaud them. When a new hire comes to the bank they learn early that chewing gum is frowned upon. An unfriendly in so many ways, Commerce Bank simply does not want gum chewing to take place in the workplace. This message is sent home in their employee orientation which is an eight-hour session focused on how to WOW the client. Kudos to Commerce Bank for understanding this unfriendly and insuring that gum chewing will not taint a customer friendly experience.

Others

There are so many other unfriendlies that we could write an entire book just on the things that anger and annoy us in the realm of customer service. Needless to say, we want to avoid the unfriendlies. Rather, we want to turn on the charm with friendlies.

Customer Friendly

There are two major practices that make a customer service experience customer friendly. The first is a conversational tone and the second are things that just make the receiving party feel good.

Conversational Tone

We begin the customer friendly process by speaking with the other person in a friendly manner. Having what I term a "conversational tone" is the key. Simply put, it is like talking to your friends and neighbors. When we are with friends, we are relaxed in our conversation and that is the atmosphere we should create during the conversation. The communication needs to remain professional, but at the same time it can be relaxed. When we speak with our neighbors the conversation ebbs and flows and in general it sounds relaxed. This is what we are striving for in the conversational tone.

Doing nice things, doing smart things

Finding opportunities to do nice things and then delivering is a huge part of customer service. For a service company performing work at a residential property, it can be as simple as picking up the newspaper at the end of the driveway and giving it to the client at the door. There are so many things that we can do that are not part of the job, but make the customer service process friendly. We should always be looking for the little things we can do to bring a smile to our clients' faces.

In July 2003, Cooper Pest Control missed an appointment with a client creating ill will. As is customary at Cooper, we stepped to the plate to solve the problem we had created. Our technician, Ron Geherty used the skills we instilled in him to provide an exceptional customer friendly experience that so inspired our client, Beverly Ferster, she sat down at her computer and composed an e-mail to me that same evening:

—Original Message—

From: xxxx@xxx.com
Sent: Tuesday, July 22, 2003 7:06 P.M.
To: Phillip D. Cooper
Subject: Rescheduled service

Hi Phil,

I had spoken with you on Saturday, July 19, when the technician did not come for monthly service. You were very accommodating by scheduling service for today, Tuesday, July 22 at 5:15p.m . . . Many people (including myself) call to complain about service (as above) and often do not take the time to praise service. I would like to compliment you for today. I've heard through the years that if a person is unhappy with something they will tell 75 people; if they are satisfied they will tell 25 people. I wonder why that is . . . .

First, thanks again for scheduling my call after work. Second, there was a very bad thunderstorm late this afternoon, including hail. I had planned on leaving work before 5p.m., but wasn't able to because of the storm. On my way home it started raining again and I was caught in traffic. Ron, my regular technician, was just turning the truck around to leave as I pulled up. It was about 5:30p.m. He patiently waited for me to get in the house.

I definitely would have to call this **WOW** service! I had thanked Ron and told him about the error in my scheduling, for the previous Saturday, and how accommodating you had been. He told me how hard you work to satisfy customers and that your company has been the best to work for (If you are hiring please let me know, I would like to send you my resume).

Just think, I was late this time and he actually waited for me! I commend you on your customer service. I have been in the service industry my entire professional life. I have always treated people the way I would **like** to be treated. This is the first time I can recall receiving that kind of treatment Thank you!

Sincerely,
Beverly Ferster

P.S. Ron told me he was leaving, he will be sorely missed! He is personable, professional and accommodating. I am serious about my resume!

WOW!!! Ron used a little common sense in recognizing that the bad weather may be impacting the client's ability to get home to meet him and combined this with the customer friendly gesture of waiting. Ron made a simple, but smart decision to wait an extra fifteen minutes, recognizing the significance this action could have. What is especially gratifying is that Ron continued to do this type of service until the day he left our organization. Ron moved to Massachusetts shortly after this visit, but during his stay with us he executed customer friendly service over and over. When Ron arrived at Cooper, his basic service skills were above average, but by the time he left, he was delivering WOW customer service time after time. Delivering customer friendly service is a standard at Cooper Pest Control and Ron's teammates are always looking for opportunities.

It is simple to achieve what Ron did for Beverly Ferster. Just look for, and practice, those little things that make others happy and you will deliver that customer friendly experience. Search for those opportunities to do the customer friendly thing and then deliver it. You will set the stage for WOW moments to occur.

Finding other Customer Friendly Opportunities — The Golden Rule of Customer Service.

Many of the customer friendly things we do are based on things we know to be just nice simple gestures; however, we must always be looking for customer friendly opportunities. Employing the Golden Rule of Customer Service with the HOW to Communicate process will take us a long way to finding these WOW nuggets.

I believe the Golden Rule of Customer Service is essential to finding those WOW nuggets and it becomes especially critical in Customer Friendly service. Remember, the Customer Service Golden Rule is

"DON'T TREAT OTHERS THE WAY YOU WANT TO BE TREATED, *TREAT THEM THE WAY THEY WANT TO BE TREATED*"

Integrating the rule into our process is simple, but we first must be on the lookout for the "ways they want to be treated." You can do this by asking questions and listening (steps eight and nine of HOW to Communicate) and when we ask questions and listen we will find things our client views as friendly. You must keep telling yourself, it is not about how we want to be treated; it is all about how the client wants to be treated. When we find those nuggets of information, we are armed with incredible tools to deliver customer friendly service.

Two-Ring Answer

There are so many customer friendly opportunities and we could write a whole book exploring them, but I want to look at one last one that I believe deserves special attention and that is the two-ring answer. The two-ring answer revolves around call centers and can make a huge impact on the effectiveness our ability to provide a WOW experience to our client. The two-ring answer is as simple as it sounds, we should answer the phone in two rings.

Marathon Data, the company which takes incredible notes, also understands the two-ring theory and their customer support staff knows nothing different. The software company, located in Oakhurst, NJ, is led by its owner and visionary, Mike Ayars. Mike is a customer service zealot and his enthusiasm emanates throughout his organization. "Our rule," says Mike "is to answer the phone in two rings, we view three rings as unacceptable." The amazing part is they do what they preach! If you are a Marathon client, you will always get the two-ring treatment.

Call the Marathon Data office and not only will you find extraordinary customer service, but rarely will the phone ring twice and when it does the "earth stops rotating" at Marathon. Their customer support team knows when the phone rings, "you jump!" The client comes first at Marathon, and business starts when the phone rings. I had the good fortune to visit their office and witness their exceptional service in action. Smiling faces are constantly answering the phones in two rings. WOW!

Ayars understands the unfriendliness that occurs when the phone rings more than once. I asked him why the attention to answering the phone on two rings. Puzzled with the question, Mike replied, "Isn't it common sense to want the phone answered quickly and promptly? Answering the phone is simply part of our basic job." Unfortunately, although Ayars is correct in the statement, that it is a basic part of the job, many companies simply do not even consider implementing this practice, let alone achieve this standard.

The other major point Mike drives home to his team through the two-ring answer is the importance of the customer, "by making sure the phone is answered within two rings has benefits beyond the one of sending a message to the customer that they are important. I like it because it reminds our staff how important the customer is every time the phone rings."

The bar that Marathon has set for itself is an extraordinary accomplishment. Yet, if you speak with their wonderful staff they view it as just the way to do business. I wish other organizations would learn from Marathon. How many times do we call places where we get the two-ring approach? Unfortunately, the answer to the question is not all that often, even worse is how many places do not even answer in three rings.

Many organizations recognizing this issue have installed automated answering of the phone in two rings, and yet, I believe they still fail in delivering the two-ring standard. The companies that have gone this route are receiving such a high volume of calls with a great diversity of potential paths that they filter the calls to the appropriate call center groups. However, if you ask the general public on how they feel about being attended to through automation, the overwhelming majority will tell you it is not customer friendly. During most WOW seminar I give, I conduct an informal survey to see who enjoys the two-ring answer by an automated attendant. Less than 25 percent of the hands go up. We are still in a society where we want a human voice to interact with and we want that voice in two rings or less. Marathon Data delivers this standard and it sets the tone for an exceptional experience.

At Cooper Pest Control, our Director of First Impressions, what the business world calls our receptionist, begins this process by answering the phone in two rings or less. We also stress the two-ring rule with the rest of our organization when a call is transferred. Do we answer every call within two rings? I wish I could tell you we are perfect, but we are not. Do we occasionally miss the mark and not pick up in two rings, the unfortunate answer is yes. But, we do not view this as acceptable and we are always striving for better solutions to insure that all calls are answered within two rings by someone who can help them. The first step in the two ring rule is to raise the bar on the expected standard and then the second step is to do it.

Remembering that the client's first impression is a lasting impression adds importance to the two-ring rule. When we do anything other than answer with a human voice in two rings we set a series of customer unfriendly emotions into place and before we even get started with the rest of the experience we have started on the wrong foot. The two-ring answer begins our process in a customer friendly way and it is that first impression that is so very important. As the old adage reads, "You never get a second chance to make a first impression."

Take the steps in your organization to institute the two ring rule. Make the two-ring rule a way of doing business as Mike Ayars has. Treat others as they want to be treated and look for those Customer Friendly nuggets to deliver to the client. Have that conversational tone as though you are speaking with your neighbor, and finally, be on the lookout for the unfriendlies. Put all of these in action and you will provide the foundation for excellent customer service.

CHAPTER 11

HOW Step 3—Smile Factor

The "Smile Factor" is a really fun and interesting step in the WOW process which is comprised of two components: the smile on our face and the smiling body. We will explore in this chapter the importance and significance of the all important smile. The second piece of the Smile Factor is what I describe as the Smiling Body or body language. We will examine the impacts of body language on the communication process and how easily body language can take the meaning of our words and turn them upside down.

The Evolution of the Smile Factor

The Smile Factor was the last piece I added to the WHAT and HOW methodology. Up until the year 2000, How to Communicate included eleven steps. In January of 2000, I was giving a WOW seminar in Virginia to a company committed to customer service, Valcourt Building Services. The company, owned by Jeff Valcourt, and a half dozen minority partners, is a window cleaning company that operates on the East Coast and is the largest private window cleaning company in the country. Valcourt understands they are not in the business of cleaning windows, but in the business of servicing their clients, which window cleaning is just one piece of the puzzle. When I went to Valcourt, the WOW system had eleven steps, when I left the Smile Factor made it 12.

Valcourt was the springboard of the Smile Factor, but how I came to that monumental moment is another story. Mike Amoroso, President of Valcourt's New Jersey operations had been present in Amelia Island in 1999 when I was asked to make the WOW presentation for the first time in public. A group of twenty other service industry companies, represented by their top executives, were present in Amelia Island for three days of casual business talk and relaxation. The trip was sponsored by The Gale Company and the leader of the trip was Bob Palestri, President of the Management Services for Gale. Bob and I were discussing the state of customer service and he was inquiring about Cooper's WOW system. Bob asked, then nudged and then gave the order that I was to make my in-house presentation to everyone in the group. Everyone assembled had to change their plans from sitting poolside with drinks in hand to listening to Phil Cooper preach about customer service. The one hour "talk" began with a group of men and women not to happy with the circumstances. After the hour was over, the mood had changed and the room was filled with a group of alive and excited faces. Mike asked if I wouldn't mind taking the talk on the road and he wanted me to deliver it to the entire Valcourt organization at their annual meeting.

The Valcourt annual meeting is much more than a gathering of officers. Instead, Valcourt takes this opportunity to gathers its managers, sales and customer service team for team building and sessions to make the company the best it can be. Saturday was WOW day and I was scheduled to give the Valcourt clan an eight-hour dose of WOW. Little did I know that my process was about to receive its final piece. We were about three hours into the seminar when I reached the Customer Friendly step and I began discussing the smile factor as part of the Customer Friendly step. Jon Capon, the President of the Washington D.C. area, walked up to me during our break and discussed a trick he used for insuring a smile, the mirror and the need for making the smile a step of its own. Jon and I discussed my reasoning for including the smile as part of the customer friendly step while Jon explained why it was so important that it should be its own step called the Smile Factor. The discussion then continued at lunch and by the time the seminar began again at 1:00 p.m., Jon's persuasive techniques won out, the WOW process had a new step.

Why did I remove it from customer friendly and elevate it to its own status. Simple, the smile is such a powerful force and as you will see, a little later in the chapter, the mirror provides a tool to measure our ability to smile. So after a bit of discussion it was obvious that Jon was onto something; it was a no-brainer that the Smile Factor should have its own place in the system.

The Smile Factor received its final facelift in the spring of 2003 and Commerce Bank provided the platform. I was attending the new employee orientation at Commerce Bank, a class they call Traditions. I am always looking to understand the top performing customer service companies in the industry and on this occasion I was observing Commerce Bank, which is turning the banking industry on its head with it wacky, but successful formula for delivering exceptional service to its clientele. During Traditions, John Manning, our trainer was discussing the smile and transitioned into a discussion on body language. Over the next twenty minutes, John discussed the importance of body language. As he spoke, I thought back to the WOW process and recognized a missing link, WOW was missing the boat on general body language.

Knowing the importance of body language and that the WOW system was missing this critical component I looked for where to place a discussion on this subject. Soon, it became evidently clear, the home for body language would be in the Smile Factor step and for good measure I know refer to body language as the Smiling Body. A smiling body is a body that sends out positive body language which enhances our opportunities to WOW.

The Smile Factor is a combination of the both a pure, unbridled smile on the face and body language that conveys and upbeat, positive attitude.

A Smile on Our Face

If we put a smile on our face, we can make the difference from us having a bad day to a tolerable day or even very good day. The smile has a tremendous mental effect on how we act and feel during our day-to-day lives. When we translate this into customer service we have a simple maxim to follow, "We always want our clients to see us with a smile."

The Smile Factor is so powerful that we can actually tell when someone is smiling even if we are not looking at them. Close your eyes and listen to someone speak. See if you can see them smiling. To test this, give them a sentence to say and ask them to say it once with a smile and once without a smile. Also, when they say the words without the smile, have them try to say the words with the same tone with the smile, but just remove the smile from their face. Now close your eyes and listen to the words and you will see what is so amazing. We can actually hear the smile.

Director of First Impressions

The Smile Factor has its greatest importance in the WOW system when someone answers the phone. When we look at organizations this becomes paramount when a company has a receptionist directing phone traffic. The receptionist only has a few brief moments to make that outstanding first impression with the caller, and the Smile Factor is the key element of WOW in making or breaking the call.

The Smile Factor is about a feeling we portray; when we smile the words have a different feel. When I think of the Smile Factor I think of Anna, our Director of First Impressions. The reception at Cooper Pest Control is very important as it is our gateway to the outside world. Anna stepped up to the plate immediately and took her WOW training to heart. When Anna started with Cooper, she was hired as a receptionist, an entry-level position in the company. Since Anna's arrival, we changed the name of her position from receptionist to Director of First Impressions and the position is no longer entry-level. The change is well deserved as Anna receives compliment after compliment regarding her phenomenal ability to always have a smile on her face.

Anna's predecessor in the position was Megan who also could smile. Megan would have her good and bad days as most of us do. During her second year with the company I was leaving for an appointment when I overheard Megan answer the phone, "Thank you for calling Cooper Pest Control, how may I direct your call." But it was not typical Megan; this morning was different, there was no smile, no smile at all. Instead the voice was flat and I was concerned. As I was walking out the door I asked Megan how she was doing. She fell into my trap and replied that it was a bad morning and she really was having a bad day on top of not feeling well.

"Megan I hope you feel better and remember to smile," was my reply as I left the office. About ten minutes later, I called the office from my cell phone and what I heard made me all warm inside. Megan answered the phone, "Thank you for calling Cooper Pest Control, how may I direct your call,", but this time the smile was radiating again.

Now I can promise you in ten minutes Megan did not miraculously feel better and I know her day had not changed significantly in 10 minutes. On the other hand, her day had changed, she was smiling again. The simple fact was she now was consciously thinking about the smile factor and was forcing herself to smile. I watched and listened to Megan the rest of the day and the smile never left her face. The simple smile makes all the difference in the world. Megan works hard at the smile factor everyday. She is conscious of its affect on people and the impact the smile has on her performance.

Anna, succeeded Megan and made an immediate impact. As I mentioned before, Anna is extraordinary and helped elevate this position. She became our Director of First Impressions. I get phone calls all of the time asking who is the person answering our phones. In a matter of a few seconds, Anna is able to set the tone for the company and set the stage for the rest of our staff. Anna is our client's first impression and what an impression she makes! One of Anna's tricks is Jon Capon's mirror and she uses it. During Anna's initial WOW training, we discussed the use of the mirror at the desk to insure the WOW smile. The next day, a mirror was at Anna's desk and has remained ever since. Keeping a mirror by your desk is the tool we need when our day is going bad or we do not feel well.

Call our office and ask our Director of First Impressions about the mirror. I promise the Director will proudly tell you it is there to remind ourselves to smile especially on the days when we are not in the mood to smile. It is her benchmark for delivering outstanding customer service. On a down day, the mirror is there to insure the smile factor is in full affect.

I cannot say enough about the smile factor and the impact it has on our everyday lives. I salute, the people in this world who walk around with a smile. Do not underestimate the Smile Factor.

The "Smiling Body"—Body Language

The "Smiling Body" is my term for non-verbal communication or what is most commonly referred to as body language. When our body smiles we are eliciting positive body language that enhances our communication process. The Smiling Body helps to deliver the WOW moment.

Studies have shown the communication process is dominated by non-verbal communication or what we commonly refer to as body language. It is estimated that body language accounts for 93 percent of the total communication process. That leaves 7 percent for verbal communication. To this point, we have focused on Verbal communication, but it becomes essential to understand the impact that body language has on our communication process.

The body language we exhibit influences dramatically the message we send when we communicate. Think about the impact the body can have on the delivery of a message. Pretend for a moment that you are working at a retail store checkout counter and a customer comes up. Smiling, you begin WOWing them and toward the end of the conversation you put your middle finger in the air. Just imagine the shock and dismay this simple action would have on the client. A simple gesture of the middle finger disrupted the entire communication process and besides destroying the WOW moment, we may have destroyed the customer relationship. Body language can turn the entire communication process on its head.

The impact of body language increases dramatically and takes on a significant role when our communication is face-to-face. Our representatives must always remember that their bodies are communicating at all times, even when they think others are not looking. So many face-to-face representatives forget this when they are not face-to-face with our clients. There have been so many times when I catch two employees exchanging negative body language when they believe no one is looking. My reaction is to wonder if they will be doing the same to me, behind my back when I leave the store. I certainly do not get the warm feeling inside when I observe this behavior.

Commerce Bank and Smiling

Commerce Bank understands the importance of the Smiling Body and during their new employee orientation they drive the point home. When you are hired by Commerce Bank, you will go through their orientation class, "Traditions." The class is all about the culture of Commerce Bank and how to WOW the client. A significant portion of the class is spent on the effects of body language. Over 90 minutes are spent showing how a smile, a gesture, or how something as simple as a yawn can send a poor message to the client. During the class I attended, the instructor John Manning had a series of rules to drive the point home. Every time he looked at you he expected a smile in return. Anyone who did not smile had to sing Karaoke to Britney Spears and in John's words, "Make the rest of us smile instead." After the first few singers, the point was well taken. Other classroom guidelines were; no resting your head on your hand and no gum chewing.

To be able to WOW our clients we must display our best body language. The Smiling Body gives us the chance to WOW and we must always remember we never know who is looking.

CHAPTER 12

How Steps 4 and 5 —

Pace And Enunciation

Soul Mates

Over the next six chapters, steps 4, 5, 6, 7, 8 and 9 are explored and are grouped together as soul mates. When I look at the WOW system there are three sets of steps that go hand-in-hand and are intricately linked. I use the soul mates to help remember the WOW system; there are three steps in the beginning, then three pairs of soul mates and finally three final steps. The Soul Mates begin with Pace and Enunciation.

HOW #4 Pace: The Metamorphosis of Pace: Speed, Inflection and Tone

Pace, the fourth step of the system underwent a metamorphosis during the first two years I developed the WOW system. When I first started, my emphasis on pace was simply on the speed of the conversation. However, as I developed the system, I recognized that along with speed were similar, but distinct components of inflection and tone. My dilemma was whether to create two additional steps for inflection and tone or to simply lump them together with speed to form Pace. To this day, I continue to struggle. It would be so easy to create five, even ten more categories in HOW. Suffice it to say I always decide that keeping the HOW in 12 manageable steps, is key to a workable system. So pace, is made up of speed, inflection and tone, and is one step in the HOW process.

Pace is the single most important verbal item in the HOW steps. Simply put, poor tone, improper inflection or a pace that is too fast or too slow can simply destroy a conversation. The intended message can be lost in the way the words were said. We can be successful in all of the other steps of WHAT + HOW and if we deliver the message with poor pace we can simply destroy what is being said. A WOW moment could become a disastrous moment if the pace of the communication is not effective.

When I think of pace, I immediately think of my daughter, Samantha, "Sami." In the summer of 1999, Samantha was approaching her sixth birthday and she was being introduced to the WHAT + HOW grading system. When Sami and I would run errands, we would listen to tapes of Cooper Pest Control's customer service representatives in the car and grade them. Samantha learned the steps of WHAT + HOW that summer.

One day, we were listening to a tape of one of our representatives, Angie, who really had a knack for hitting the marks in inflection. As we listened to Angie speak to one of our clients, I asked Samantha what she thought. "What great emphasis, dad!" I thought for a second and asked her what she had meant. I never really thought of Pace as having emphasis. Samantha's reply remains with me as if she said it yesterday, "Dad, don't you hear? The words are coming to life, she has such great emphasis!"

Simply put, Samantha summed up the concept of speed, inflection and tone, the basis for what I call pace. We could simply look at pace as the speed of the words coming out of the mouth. Instead, I like to look at pace as a finely balanced soup of speed, inflection and tone coming altogether to form the pace of the conversation.

Speed

The speed which we say our words is the foundation of pace. Our words can be just right or they can be too fast or too slow. We are looking for a nice rhythm to the words. Conversely, without rhythm, I always think of a metronome going back and forth keeping a steady beat—the beat if not changed, will simply mesmerize us and put us to sleep. A flat pace is comparable to the metronome.

How fast is too fast and how slow is too slow? It can be very subjective and it is also a product of the receiving party. For instance, if I am speaking to a foreigner whose English is weak I need to slow down the speed of my words. But, I have to be careful not to become monotone. Conversely, if I am in New York City, the speed of my words will pick-up. Simply put, New Yorkers in general have a little extra zip in their words.

What is important is that the receiving party can understand what you are saying, and has enough time to process the words in their mind. Speed, when used properly, adds life to the conversation; a good rhythm keeps the receiving party's attention.

Speed is specifically linked to the soul mate of pace, enunciation. We will explore this in greater detail in the next chapter, but how fast or slow we talk will impact how clearly our words are understood. By slowing our pace someone who is having trouble understanding our words will have an easier time making the correct interpretation.

The basics of speed are very simply how fast the words come out of our mouth. We can either talk very fast or we can talk very s-l-o-w-l-y. When I think of someone speaking fast, I pretend I am listening to a radio advertisement for a car dealer and at the beginning or end of the advertisement the disclaimers being read at a very fast pace, are almost inaudible. We have all heard these advertisements and the super speed at which the words are being said. On the flip side there is slow. When I think of slow I think of someone who words are so slow you just want to rip the words out of the person's mouth. When you are listening to this type person there is the tendency to get fidgety and not really hear what the person has to say.

In the search of effective speed we want to be right in the middle, not too fast and not too slow and at the same time we want to vary our speed. As we vary our speed, we develop a rhythm to the conversation and this is what we are striving for. We should be able to clearly understand the words that are being said and be able to digest the meaning of the words. The speed at which the words are being said goes a long way towards achieving this goal.

In addition, to the speed at which we speak, the words; we must consider the effective use of a pause in the conversation. Many of us get to a point when we could pause, but instead we use the word "UM." For those of us who get a case of the Ums it is a very hard habit to break. If we are going to be customer service professionals it is very important that we work tirelessly in eliminating UM from our vocabulary. We want to replace the UM with an effective pause. Doing so positively affects the speed of the conversation.

Ultimately, what we are left with is occasional pauses in our speech pattern that allow both the listener and the person speaking with a quick chance to gather their thoughts.

The effective use of speed simply revolves around speaking with a rhythm that incorporates pauses and a range of speed, while avoiding speaking too fast or too slow. By accomplishing this, the conversation becomes very easy to listen to and provides a platform to shine in other areas.

Inflection

Bringing words to life, as Samantha so aptly puts it, is the basis for inflection. We can make words sound BIG or we can make them sound *small*. Have you ever heard an excellent story teller? What makes them so special is their ability to make the story come to life. Speed and inflection are the major tools in their toolkit.

Listening to others deliver a message with excellent inflection is a wonderful experience. Take a moment to stop into a bookstore and listen to a book reading or someone reading poetry. Bringing words to life is such a memorable experience. One of the best ways to see this, is to watch someone reading to a child and observing the difference in the child's attention span when someone reads to them with excellent inflection versus no inflection. When the words come to life, the children listen with rapt attention. We can make language jump to life with a little touch here, a swoosh of emphasis there, a pause, a crescendo or decrescendo. It is very much like a symphony, but using words as the music.

When you emphasize the words, your chances of the receiving party hearing everything you have to say is much greater. Their mind is less apt to wander as you say what you are saying. By gaining their focus, the opportunity for better comprehension on the receiver's part is present.

Inflection and L.L. Bean

Understanding the use of inflection can again be demonstrated by picking apart a conversation we had with Maureen from L.L. Bean. I play the Maureen audio in many seminars as great example of WHAT + HOW. When reading the words below the emphasis is on the words in bold. The conversation went,

Nancy: Hi, I was just wondering if you can send me a clothing catalog and more specifically do you have children's catalogs?

Maureen: Yes, Yes.

Nancy: OK, if you could send me one I'd appreciate it.

Maureen: Oh, It would give me great joy to do that, I love our kid's catalog.

I wish you could hear the tape. When Maureen says the words "great joy" and "love" they just come to life. In fact, you really believe Maureen is going to receive great joy by sending the catalog.

Funny enough, when I give seminars and the conversation is played, not everyone agrees with me on this point. Occasionally, I will play the conversation and someone's reaction is that Maureen sounds too hokey. Personally, I have found this opinion to be in the minority. Most people listening to Maureen hear what I hear, sincerity and words with meaning. With emphasis, the words come to life, and when we grade Maureen, you will learn more about grading later, she earns a 10 for pace on a scale of 1 to 10.

The intent of Maureen's words take on a whole

different meaning if we change the emphasis on the words. Imagine the conversation if Maureen has changed around her inflection and emphasis by emphasizing the words in bold.

"Oh, it would **give** me great joy to do **that,** I love our kid's **catalog.**"

By emphasizing GIVE, THAT and CATALOG the sentence does not flow and seems out of place. Our ability to focus on what is being is lessened and instead of comprehending what is being said, we are focused on trying to unravel the emphasis on words that would not normally be emphasized.

To this day, I find inflection to be the most fascinating part, when I tape myself. Listening and analyzing the words I have chosen to emphasize and then determining if I delivered the message I intended is a fascinating exercise. Sometimes my communication is very effective and other times it could be improved upon. However, taping and grading myself allows me to improve my ability to emphasize words effectively.

Tape yourself and listen to your words and your inflection. What words are you emphasizing? Did you get the desired effect? Do you emphasize the right words? It is quite amazing how you can change the whole context of the conversation. Repeat some of the same sentences in your tape and alter the emphasis and see if you can achieve a better result. What you will find will surprise you.

Tone

By changing the emphasis on words, we change the meaning of our sentence. In addition, the meaning of the word can be completely changed with the tone we use. The same word can have multiple meanings simply by how we say it. If we are in a lousy mood and our tone reflects our mood, the words take on a different meaning. When we are grading tone, we are asking ourselves a simple question, "Does the tone we are using, matched with the words we choose, deliver the message we intend?"

Imagine a basketball coach infuriated with an official's call. The coach wishes to lash out at the referee and make an impact. This is a coach known for tirades and in this case he wants to be heard. The coach runs over to the referee, hands waving in the air and in a very soft, reassuring tone says "What were you thinking when you made that call?" My guess is the referee would be a bit bewildered. Why soft, quiet words, where we are expecting loud, staccato, barking words? The tone sets up the impression we desire to make.

The proper tone becomes critical in delivering superior customer service. Our tone needs to be upbeat and positive. We want to send the message through our tone that we are in control of the process and in control of our emotions.

Problem resolution is an area of customer service that is completely dependent on the tone of the conversation. My definition of problem resolution is when I am speaking with an unhappy client and my goal is to make them into a life-long client. By insuring that the tone of conversation is upbeat and positive and by avoiding a condescending tone, we give ourselves a chance of delivering the proper message. By altering the tone, we will either further enrage the client or begin to diffuse the situation. If we become defensive and our voice takes on a tone of arrogance, we will lose the battle. Instead, the tone must be soft and reassuring without patronizing or being condescending. The tone must send a vote of confidence that we are in control of the situation.

Insuring consistent tone is the challenge of all

customer service representatives. This becomes especially important when the representative is having bad day. The customer service representative who is not a professional wears their emotions on their sleeve and when they are having a bad day, tone is one of the first things to go wrong after losing the smile factor. The best customer service representatives learn how to control their tone regardless of how they are feeling. Our personal emotions should not be part of the conversation and as hard as it is, we must strive to insure that poor tone does not creep into our conversations.

Conclusion about Pace

Speed, inflection and tone. When you put them all together you have the pace of the conversation. These three factors that make up pace, take on huge significance in delivering the message we desire. You can take the most impressive conversation, score high marks on all aspects of WHAT + HOW and with poor pace ruin the conversation. So, the bottom line is to have nice rhythm, while using speed and inflection to bring words to life plus giving the words the desired meaning and a tone that sends the message in a positive and upbeat fashion. Putting it all together is the key and will insure that the rest of your message will be heard correctly.

HOW #5: Enunciation

The soul mate to Pace is Enunciation, which is the product of two things, our accent or dialect in relation to the listening party and how clearly we say our words. The Merriam-Webster dictionary defines enunciation as, "to utter articulate sound." It is being able to understand the words clearly, that matters. Have you ever had a conversation with someone who sounds like they have marbles in their mouth? How about someone who is talking to you while chewing gum? These factors and so many more affect our ability to enunciate clearly.

Dialect is a very personal thing, but when it comes to communication it is so very important to make sure that the receiving party understands what is occurring. In recent years, some technology companies have created technical help call centers in other parts of the world. The people they hire are very savvy and bright and can deliver outstanding technical advice.

The problem occurs when they do not adjust their communication to the receiving party. If I have a technology company and I set up a technical help call center in India, it becomes critical that my staff adjust to the people that they are speaking to. The representative will have to slow down the speed and carefully enunciate the words so, the listening party, can clearly understand what is being said.

However, what so often happens is that the representative does not change the enunciation. The end result is a client who is working so hard to understand what is being said that they are unable to effectively listen to the message. The client becomes frustrated and no matter how good the knowledge of that person is, or how nice they are, the message is not understood and therefore the rest is inconsequential.

Tech Help Goes To India

Accents become especially important when the customer service representative has a different accent than the receiving party. A great example of how accents can affect customer service is looking at Dell Computer and their customer service. In the summer of 2002, I had a problem with my computer and made a call to the technical help line. Over the next three days, I called the help desk three times and each time I reached someone with a very thick foreign accent. It was such a wretched experience that I simply wanted to scream. I was having such difficulty understanding the person I was speaking to that I wanted to hang up the phone. There were so many times that I asked the representative to repeat himself, you would think he would have gotten the message.

Enunciation in a Multi-Cultural Society

Accents and dialects is not just a product of different nationalities, it can be as simple as different parts of the United States. If I put a New Yorker in Mississippi and she does not change her speed and enunciation in relation to the Southern dialect her message will be lost. Of course, I do not expect the New Yorker to sound like a southerner, but what I do expect is to slow down the speed so the words are clearly understood. However, I must be careful not to slow it down so that I insult the other party.

Whether you are in a national call center or dealing with the citizens of one town, enunciation is critical. Each conversation will be slightly different. There is such a wide diversity in the population in the United States and because of the world economy; we speak to people with different accents and dialects all day long. Therefore, we have no choice, but to adjust. It is our job as the representative to adjust—it should not be up to the clients to adjust.

Again, this is where taping comes in to the process. We should tape a number of conversations and then play them back to see if we adjust our enunciation from call to call. If the accents of our clients are different, but we do not change our enunciation, chances will be that our client may be having trouble understanding what we are saying. By taping the conversation and hearing how we have adjusted the enunciation of our words, we will become better at making these adjustments. When we listen to the tape, we are looking for cues from the client that helps to indicate whether they are having trouble following our conversation. When asking questions of the client, we should listen carefully to our client's voice to determine if they sound confused. If confusion is evident, it may be indicative of our poor enunciation.

Are you Enunciating Effectively?

Another key indicator is when the receiving party asks you to repeat what you said. Sometimes you are asked to repeat your words because the other party was not paying attention. More often than not, the real reason, is that you did not enunciate your words clearly enough or there was a problem with the pace of the conversation. This is why pace and enunciation are soul mates as they impact each other greatly. We need to work hard to remember that enunciation will change from conversation to conversation and it is up to us to insure that the receiving party can clearly understand what is being said.

CHAPTER 13

HOW Steps 6 and 7—

Pronouns and Use Of Names

Our second set of soul mates is Pronouns and the Use of Names. They are soul mates because they both tied to how we reference the other party. We help insure the success of the conversation by using correct pronouns and using the client's name throughout the conversation to show we are aware of who they are. Using the proper pronouns and names appears to be simple, but in many cases this simple task becomes a difficult habit for representatives to do consistently.

HOW #6: Proper Use of Pronouns

As with the other steps in the HOW process, Pronouns is actually made up of a number of sub-items. A number of different factors meld together when looking at pronouns. We will see the effect the word THEY has on the conversation and how we integrate I, we, us, into our conversational vocabulary. We will look at how we reference a third party during the conversation and how we reference a department or another organization. Finally we will examine how we reference objects, such as a computer, during the conversation.

Each of these four items is distinct, and unique. When viewing pronouns we begin by thinking of good pronouns and bad pronouns. I, we, us, are the pronouns I love. The word THEY is a bad pronoun and should be stricken from the customer service dictionary.

The Four Letter Word of Customer Service—THEY

T-H-E-Y, is the four-letter word of customer service. Whenever I think of THEY, I think of a time when I had my assistant, Nancy Kintner call one of the leading computer manufacturers to check on one of my orders. The call went like this:

Computer Guy:	*"OK, Is this for Phil Cooper Pest Control, Inc."*
Nancy:	*"Yes."*
Computer Guy:	*"Um, no I just have on the seventeenth that they're both back ordered, but THEY have not fulfilled it yet and I am pretty certain THEY'RE still holding off on the mini-docks because I have not seen them on recent orders."*
Nancy:	*"OK."*
Computer Guy:	*"So, it should be coming in relatively quickly here, I don't know exactly when, but THEY'RE telling us for both parts sometime around the first of March."*
Nancy:	*"OK then a week later we should probably get them?"*
Computer Guy:	*"Exactly. Maybe a little less than that."*
Nancy:	*"OK, Alrighty, thanks."*
Computer Guy:	*"Goodbye."*

Count the number of THEY or THEY'RE in the conversation, an incredible three times in three sentences. As I listened to the conversation played back, I scratched my head wondering who the customer service representative was referring to. I was kind of shocked and dismayed at the conversation since this company had recently won a number of customer service awards. But to prove a point I went one step further. I called the corporate headquarters of this leading computer manufacturer and reached the receptionist. The conversation went like this:

RECEPTION: "Hello, [name of company] how may I direct your call?"
PHIL COOPER: "Can I speak to THEY?"
RECEPTION: "Excuse me sir, we do not have any THEY'S who work here, if you give me a name or a department, I would be happy to connect you."
PHIL COOPER: "I do not have a name; I would like to speak to THEY."
RECEPTION: "Sir, I really would like to help you, but I need you to work with me. Can you give me a name or a department?"
PHIL COOPER: "As I said before, I unfortunately do not have a name or a department. Can you connect me to THEY?"
RECEPTION: "Sir, I do not find you funny, I need a name or a department."
PHIL COOPER: "OK, why don't you tell me who I need to speak with?"

And with that, I took my tape recorder with the conversation between Nancy and the Customer Service for the company and clicked it on. When I brought the phone back to my ear the receptionist was no longer there, and the phone was ringing to what ended up being the Customer Service Department.

WOW, this receptionist really did not like me and I did feel bad about taking it out on her the way I did. But let me ask a simple question. Who was I supposed to ask for? Remember all I knew was "THEY have not fulfilled it yet" and "THEY'RE still holding off on the mini-docks" AND "THEY'RE telling us . . . ." Who in the world is THEY? For all I know it could be a distribution center in South Dakota, a fulfillment center in Texas or a manufacturing center in Asia. It could have been the man in the moon or Froofie the dog. Unless I am a mind reader, I have no idea who the computer guy was referring to. I am not even sure if "they" actually works with the same company. All I needed was a name or a department to refer to when calling the receptionist and instead I was holding onto that ugly, four letter word that makes me shudder, they.

Think of the conversation and substitute words the customer service agent could have used. It could have gone something like this.

"The fulfillment center in Houston is indicating the order is not fulfilled yet and the center is still holding on the mini-docks . . . . and they are telling us . . . ."

Now, would I prefer to have a person's name at the fulfillment center or more information? Absolutely! But at the very minimum, I have a place to begin with the receptionist. Instead, I had a receptionist who thought I was a complete jerk. Now in some of my friends' circles when I relate this story they agree, but most people just laugh and laugh hard because the people who hear it have had their own "they experience."

The word, they, can actually be used in a conversation and not be a four letter word. You will notice that in the better example, I still used the word "they" one time, "They are telling us." The word they can actually be used in proper context if it proceeds a name of a person or a department. Actually, this is what is grammatically correct and by using the rules of English grammar we can occasionally use the word THEY without it becoming a four letter word.

Striking the word they from our vocabulary is a very difficult thing to do because we are so accustomed to using it. They is most commonly used when we are put in a difficult position or we are required to say something to the client we do not agree with. So many times, this occurs when we lack information or have to enforce a policy or procedure we are not comfortable with. I love to listen to difficult clients and observe the real customer service professionals. If you carefully listen, the word they will never be used, since sprinkled in will be other pronouns and names.

If you use THEY a lot in your speech it is a hard habit to break. Just talk to Mike Mullen. Mike is a fantastic representative of Cooper Pest Control, Inc. who works hard to break the "they habit." Mike is super on the phone, but during his first year with the company his greatest hurdle was striking the word they from his vocabulary. Mike is a true professional and cares about his craft; however, every so often the word they would slip into the conversation. On Mike's wall is the word THEY, with a big circle around it and a diagonal line through it as a constant reminder of the word. Mike, being the consummate professional, works hard every day to insure that the four-letter word does not creep into his conversations. He also knows how easy it is to use "they," especially if the call becomes difficult. The trick, as Mike knows, is to constantly be on guard to avoid using the word and replacing it with names of people or departments.

I, We, Us

Thankfully, there are good pronouns which we should use. My favorites are I, we and us as well as sprinkling in the name of the department of a specific reference to a third party. By doing this, we make the conversation personal and we provide the receiving party with valuable information that they can reference later on. The word I is a very powerful conversational tool. When we use the word I, we are taking responsibility and accountability for the outcome of the conversation and it will help gain the trust of the other party. The pronoun, "we" is also a powerful pronoun. If I am speaking with a client and use the word we in the conversation, it implies that I am part of a bigger whole and my teammates and I are one cohesive group. We insinuates that we are working together for a common goal. The word we, as with I, will help gain the respect and trust of the client. The pronoun, us, has a very similar impact to using we. Putting all of these pronouns together in a conversation can have a tremendous impact on the client. Let's look at two conversations, the first with I, we, us and the second without these words.

An Average Call

Client: "Can you tell me when I might receive my book in the mail."

Rep: "They are telling me that it will ship in three days and if it does not reach you by Friday you should call back and let us know."

Good Use of I, We, Us

Client: "Can you tell me when I might receive my book in the mail."

Rep: "*I am looking at the shipping information and the book should reach you by Friday. **I** am confident that you will receive it on time, but if **you** have other questions you can call **me** back. If **I** am not available, one of **my** teammates will be sure to help you. As **I** mentioned before **my** name is Mike Jones . . . ."*

The call takes on a whole different tone and feel when we insert the pronouns I and MY into our conversation. The client knows who is able to help them and we know there is accountability for the call. In a world of impersonal customer service, the use of proper pronouns can make the difference between an average customer service call and an above average experience for the client.

Reference to a Third Party's Name

Referring to a third party in vague terms will also impact the conversation in a negative fashion. Here is a great way to understand this, is by the following example.

CLIENT (Mrs. Jones):   "Can you tell me when you will be coming to my house?"

Rep: "THEY are indicating that HE will be arriving between 10 and 11 o'clock."

Instead, we could make this much more customer friendly by inserting the third party's name instead of they. By doing this we get the following:

Rep: "Yes I can Ms. Jones. Ron, our technician, is indicating on his dispatch that he will be arriving between 10 and 11 o'clock."

The difference between the two is startling and shows what a few extra words can do. In the good example, we start of by saying "yes I can." The use of I shows that I am taking responsibility for the call and I'm not going to pass the buck. This will be extremely important as we look to gain the trust of the client. We proceed to say "Ron, our technician," and again we avoid the use of they by inserting Ron's name and then referring to his department. We accentuate this by adding the word "OUR" to the sentence in an effort to take accountability and gain the trust of the client.

Customer service representatives who are handling problem resolution calls must remember not to use THEY. Think about a time when someone was yelling at you about a problem they were having and referring to a prior conversation that you knew to be incorrect. Many people would become defensive and say, "I don't know why they said this to you." It is just how we typically respond. They is an easy way to shift the blame to others and when the problem is not our fault the use of they increases. We should never shift the blame, instead our objective is to accept the problem as our own and use pronouns that show the client that we are taking control of the problem. We will explore this further in the chapter on problem resolution. Just remember, T-H-E-Y is a four-letter word, the four-letter bad word in customer service.

Inanimate Objects

The reference to inanimate objects during a conversation as if they are flesh and blood drives me insane. Have you ever called somewhere and the person says, "The computer is telling us . . ." Well, as of the writing of this book, computers were not speaking to us yet. The computer did not speak to us. Instead we were interpreting information that we were seeing on a monitor. A much nicer, softer way of saying the same thing is "According to my information we are . . . ." The use of my makes the conversation much more personal and puts you in charge. It is YOUR information, not the computers.

As with the word THEY, customer service representatives refer to inanimate objects when the pressure is on. This especially happens when the representative is not comfortable with the technology they are using. For example if the representative is using software that is new and is difficult to navigate you will so often hear the representative talking about the computer as if it were a living object. The bottom line is that inanimate objects do not talk and we should never refer to objects in these terms. The computer is a source that provides our representatives with information. Once we gain the information it is the representative's responsibility to take accountability for the information and to insure that the client gains the trust of our organization from this accountability.

Putting Pronouns together

Every other week at Cooper Pest I will send a WOW reminder to my teammates to help them keep the WOW edge. One of my favorites was titled "The They Syndrome" I will share it with you because I think it captures the essence of Pronouns and brings everything together.

> It is important to be on guard for the "THEY SYNDROME." This syndrome is a common malady when we become frustrated with another part of the company. Common causes for this malady are: a mistake by another group in the company (technicians, sales, accounting) that impacts the client and then the client takes it out on us, a mistake by a teammate, improper communication by management about a policy.
>
> The THEY malady is most common during our busy season although it can occur

anytime during the year. When we get a case of the THEY'S the receiving party of the conversation will see a company that is not cohesive and is pointing fingers at each other.

Curing the malady takes hard work and perseverance. Instead of using the word they, remember to do the following:

Avoid Bad Pronouns: THEY, THEIR, INANIMATE OBJECT ("the computer says")

Use good pronouns: I, WE, US, ME, YOU, YOU'RE

The Rule of THEY: You can use the word they, but only if it is referring back to a subject.

Here are some examples to help you.

Bad: I am not sure when **THEY** will arrive at the house

Good: I am not sure when **OUR TECHNICIAN** will arrive,

Better: I am not sure when **YOUR TECHNICIAN BEN**, will arrive at **YOUR** house

Bad: The people you need to speak with are all on the phones and **I** am not sure when **THEY** will be free, can **I** transfer you to **THEIR** voice mail

Good: OUR Specialists are all helping other clients and I am not sure when **THEY** will be free, would **YOU** prefer to hold, have **ME** take a message or go to **OUR** specialists voice mail.

Better: Our Specialists, Mike and Janice are helping other clients and **I** am not sure when one of **THEM** will be free. Ms. Client would **YOU** prefer to hold, have **ME** take a message or go to **OUR** specialists voice mail?

Remember, the rule of THEY. It is OK if it is grammatically correct. In the good example, THEY refers back to OUR SPECIALISTS which is the subject and in the Better example, THEIR also refers back to Specialist.

Bad: THE COMPUTER says that **YOU** are scheduled for next Tuesday between 8 and 10 am

Good: I see **YOU** are on the schedule for next Tuesday between 8 and 10 am

Better: I see **YOU** are on **OUR** schedule for next Tuesday between 8 and 10 am

Start practicing this. **When taping and grading this week** be sure to pay special attention to your use of pronouns.

Remember:

- *When you are speaking with someone, remember not to get a case of the THEY'S. This malady is waiting to infect you . . .*

- *The malady can become epidemic at this time of year so be on your guard.*
- *If you do say THEY try and understand what caused it and how you could have said the sentence in a different way.*

HOW #7 Names

Step number seven, "Names," sounds simple, but has lots of subtle complexities. However, there is one consistent theme, "Names are important and the caller should only have to say their name once." As we explore the use of names in the conversation, keeping this commitment is paramount in the effort to deliver that WOW moment.

Although much of the use of names seems to be common sense, I find this area to be one of the more controversial and philosophical steps within the WHAT + HOW system. Each organization I work with has to make clear decisions on how to utilize names and then effectively communicate it to their entire team. How we obtain the client's name is the first nuance and then the decision on whether to use the client's first or last name forms the second organizational decision.

When using names in a conversation we should always be following three simple rules.

> ➢ *Rule 1: Write down the person's name phonetically as soon as they say it and pronounce it correctly.*
> ➢ *Rule 2: Use the name at least twice during the conversation, once at the beginning and once at the end.*
> ➢ *Rule 3: Mix in the name sporadically throughout the conversation, but do not overuse the name.*

However, before we can use the rules we must first get the client's name and although this sounds straight forward, it is not as clear-cut as it may seem.

Even before repeating the name, there are some things that will help to insure that we do not slip during this step. Most customer service representatives should get in the habit of writing down the client's name when the conversation begins. I am a believer in asking for the client's name at the very beginning of the conversation. In fact, asking for the client's name is the very first question we ask at Cooper Pest Control, if we do not know who is on the line when we pick it up. We always start off by saying:

Cooper representative:	*"Hi my name is [name] can I please have your name?"*
Client:	*"This is John Aadamonson."*
Cooper representative:	*"John, may I please have your street address?"*

There are many things to look at regarding this opening statement. Why the use of the first name, where is the company's name, and why have we used our name first? All of these are important points that should be and will be explored. But before we dive into the world of names this is a good time to look at the Director of First Impressions at Cooper Pest Control or what is commonly known as the receptionist.

The Director of First Impressions— The Beginning of the Call at Cooper Pest

At Cooper Pest, our Director of First Impressions sets the tone for the caller's experience. We take this position very seriously at Cooper, but there was a time when we did not. For years, our office staff simply answered the phones when it rang. We had a small team of four people in the office and the all of the lines would ring at everyone's desk. Whoever could pick up the line first would begin with, "Thank you for calling Cooper Pest Control, this is Phil can I please have your name?" . . . For many years, this method worked fine, but eventually we decided to move to a receptionist, where one person fields all of the calls for the company and distributes them out.

As I looked at moving to a receptionist, the larger question was whether I should introduce automated attendant or have a live voice on the line when our clients call in. I stand firm that although it costs significantly more dollars to have a live person answer the phone, I am willing to make the investment. The only time you will get an automated attendant is when the call volume outstrips our ability to answer the calls in three rings.

So, in 1999, I took the plunge and created the receptionist position at Cooper Pest Control. Armed with the knowledge that we were going to use a person as for our first impression to our clients, I researched to see how other companies handle this role. Over the years, I had met successful business owners utilizing receptionists and I took note of a handful of the companies with exceptional receptionists. As I explored the exceptional receptionists, I found one common thread. These business owners did not view reception as an entry-level position and they were paying top dollar for their receptionists. I knew what I needed to do, create a high level position to answer the phones. I then proceeded to make a tragic mistake, I gave in to my fiscal side and became nervous over the money I would need to spend to hire the type of person who could deliver the quality I knew was important. I began to consider the reception position as an entry-level role with an entry-level wage. I discussed this with my

Human Resource Manager, Robin Morgan and we convinced ourselves that this was the correct decision. We would learn what a tragic mistake this was.

First, we brought in temps and then a few new hires. Was it WOW? No it was YUK!!! I would go by the reception area and shudder as I would listen to the first impression people calling our office were receiving.

In the summer of 2000, we made a great new hire, Megan Rigney. Megan was a gamble, an 18 year old looking for an entry-level position and we hired her as our receptionist. Megan went through WOW training and she was the first person I witnessed at Cooper performing the position the way it was meant to be performed. A year later, an opportunity within the Business Development team presented itself and we offered the position to Megan. During the time Megan was in the reception position we continued treating it as entry-level although we were fortunate to have her do an outstanding job. But as I looked at this more closely, I began to recognize the mistake we had made the first time and how difficult it was to find Megan. I also thought about the damage we had inflicted on our clients during the steady stream of receptionists before Megan arrived.

Enter Anna Andrews. Now, to begin with, topping the job Megan was doing would be quite a feat. Megan at reception was outstanding. Megan will fill in for Anna from time-to-time to this day. What we have with Anna, well it goes beyond words, and it has changed my perception on the importance of this position forever.

The first major change was to elevate the position of reception from entry-level to a skilled position with commensurate pay. The second major change was to change to the title of the position from reception to The Director of First Impressions, and it is the first impression that Anna makes on our callers that sticks with them. I must get a call a week from someone asking who we have answering our phones and letting me know how lucky we are to have such an excellent member of our team. Anna is that good. It starts with the smile factor and works its way through all 12 steps of how, the five steps of what and the ten objectives of WOW. Anna understands WHAT + HOW and the investment pays for itself everyday. Whether it is Anna on the phone or one of our staff filling in, you will find an outstanding first impression when calling our office. I challenge you to call any day, a simple dial of 800-949-2667 and see if we are on our toes, are we ready for game day. The Director of First Impressions sets the tone for WHAT + HOW and it begins with getting the caller's name.

Getting the caller's name

How we handle obtaining the caller's name and then how we use it becomes extremely important in developing the first impression of the caller. To illustrate the nuances, let's revisit Anna and how she handles calls that come into our office.

Anna: "Good morning, thank you for calling Cooper Pest Control how may I direct your call?"
Caller: "I would like to speak with Phil Cooper."
Anna: "Can I please have your name?"
Caller: "Yes, Harry Jones."
Anna: "Thank you, I will transfer you now."

In this situation, since the caller is asking for an individual, Anna calls that person's office and announces the call. "Phil, I have Harry Jones on the line for you" and once I acknowledge that I can take the call, she transfers it to me. What happens next when I answer the phone is very important in the world of customer service. Do I answer the call as many people would, "Hello, Phil Cooper," and then pause, or do I answer, "Hello Mr. Jones, this is Phil Cooper." Stop and think for a second about the differences between the two responses. In the first response, our Director of First Impressions asked Mr. Jones for his name and he gave it to her. Anna then called my office and told me his name, but when I answered the phone I did not repeat the name back. I firmly believe this sends a poor message to the party that has called. Why should Anna have asked for the name if I was not going to acknowledge it when I answer my line?

My advice to companies with receptionists is to stop asking for the caller's name if your staff is not going to acknowledge the name when they take the call. This simple change can dramatically change the impression the caller has before reason for the call begins. Starting the call off on the right foot is so very important and how we ask for a name and then we use it is so very important.

Varying opinions on how we answer the phone

As I have traveled around the country and discussed the topic of answering the initial call, I have learned how many differing opinions there are regarding this initial step when the phone rings. The greatest point of contention is whether the Director of First Impressions should ask for the caller's name or simply transfer the call. Many customer service experts will advise against asking for the name up front and with good reason, if the receptionist asks for a name there can be the impression that all calls are being screened which turns many people off. In the above conversation, if I stepped out of my office and Anna realizes I am not there and she tells Mr. Jones I am not available, even though it is a legitimate reason, since I am not in my office, it may seem that I screened the call. The message it sends to Mr. Jones is that I know who is on the line and he is not important enough to speak to at the moment. This certainly is not a WOW message to send to the caller. There are times when we genuinely cannot get on the call, we are in meetings or we forgot to press the button on the phone indicating we are not available or a host of other reasons. Regardless of why, the danger we face when asking for the name up front is a poor impression.

The flip side are the advantages we get by Anna asking the name and what she is able to do with the inbound calls on a consistent basis. It now becomes a warm personal conversation, especially if the person is waiting to speak with someone. Anna manages the call and finds out what the caller wishes to do, keeps them informed as to what is happening with the party they are trying to reach and mixes in their name. I strongly believe that arming Anna with the caller's name outweighs the negatives of the asking for the name.

The decision we reached at Cooper is that it is more important to arm Anna with the name so she can provide the personal touch, by using client's name than the poor impression we make when the call is eventually transferred to voice mail instead. Of course, we inform the person first that the person they are trying to reach is not available and ask if they would like their voice mail.

What happens next at Cooper is the real key. Once Anna announces the call, what does the person receiving the call do? I love to watch people and other organizations. Time after time, person after person the same mistake is repeated again and again.

"Hi this is Phil Cooper," or worse "Hi this is Phil Cooper can I please have your name?" Ouch!!!! Remember that Anna called my office and announced the person as Harry Jones. It is my job to make sure I remember who I am speaking to, and most importantly, let the caller know that the question our Director of First Impressions asked, "Can I please have your name" was not a waste. This is such a critical point. If anyone in the organization has asked the name of the caller and we are in possession of the name, we should never ever ask for it again. This goes for reception transferring a call or simply one person transferring to another person. It is up to the transferring party to announce the name and for the person in Cooper taking the call to announce the name when they answer the call.

If I am not familiar with the caller I will answer, "Hello Harry, this is Phil Cooper how can I help you?" Every time I do this with someone I do not know, I love to sit back and listen to their reaction. It can be amusing at times because they simply are not prepared to have the phone answered this way. The fact that I have addressed them by their name right off the bat perplexes them, but makes for a comfortable conversation.

The other possibility is that I am familiar with the caller, and I will change my opening slightly to "Hi Harry how can I help you?" Depending on how well I know the person, I may make it less informal, but I always start with their name. Remember the commitment "Names are important and the caller should only have to say their name once." Keeping that commitment is critical, but while keeping it another critical factor is pronouncing the name correctly and then remembering the name.

Rule I: Writing down the name and pronouncing it correctly

Remembering and pronouncing names is the first step in using names correctly. As simple as this seems, it is often abused and ignored by the world of customer service. For those of you who have tough names to pronounce you know exactly what I mean. I am shocked and dismayed at how the people with difficult names just simply give up and accept that most people are just going to screw up their name on a regular basis.

I remember in grade school, the teacher reading out the names on the first day of class and butchering many of the names. What I most remember is a few of the teachers who would stop and ask the student to say their name first and one of two things would happen. Either the teacher would commit the pronunciation to memory or would write it down. In either case, the impression on the student was significant since it was rare that it ever happened. This is no different in our everyday lives, but what makes my skin crawl is that customer service representatives have the opportunity every time to hear the pronunciation of the name, and yet in so many cases, they waste away the opportunity and then turn around, and butcher the name.

It takes work to insure that we pronounce names correctly, and that we remember how to pronounce the name. Take For instance, a friend of mine who spells her name Marianne. Now I would expect that most of you would pronounce her name Mary-Ann and if you were to do so you would be way wrong. You see Marianne is actually a Danish name pronounced My-anna. There are so many times when I am with her and her name is not pronounced correctly, and she shrugs it off. However, I am certain it means a lot when someone goes out of their way to insure the proper pronunciation of her name. I can give you another example. Alicia works with Muller Interiors in New Jersey. Once again, you would be shocked at what people do to Alicia's name. There are two ways to say Alicia; A-lish-a or A-leesh-a. When I met Alicia and she introduced herself as A-leesh-a, I immediately made a mental note and then looked at her business card to see how it was spelled. Over the months that I have worked with Alicia, I continue to be amazed at the number of people who should pronounce her name correctly that do not and say it as A-lish-a. What is also intriguing is that Alicia allows this to happen. One day I asked her about it, and she said it just is simply too much effort to correct people and it really does not matter. But, with a little more digging, I uncovered when someone takes the time to pronounce it correctly it has a positive impact on her.

We have already examined two difficult names, Marianne and Alicia. But the problem can occur with simple names like Lori and Laurie. Many people pronounce the name the same, but if you ask these two women if there is a difference, the answer is a simple, Yes!!! Lori, is phonetically L-OR-EE; Laurie is L-AWR-EE. If you can make the distinction, it makes a tremendous impact on the caller.

The point to take home is that we need to get the name and then pronounce it correctly over and over. A real simple problem in customer service is that the caller says their name; we repeat it back and then later in the conversation realize we have forgotten the name. In order to be able to repeat the name back, we have to insure that we do not forget it. Some people have razor sharp memories and instant playback. To you, my hats off and you can skip the next few paragraphs. Most of us in this world are like me, you have a pretty good memory, but it's not perfect. Therefore, there are a few tricks to insure that we remember the name and then say it correctly.

There is nothing worse than realizing that you have forgotten the name. It is embarrassing to ask the name again and sends the message to the client that you are not paying attention to them. My trick is to write the name down on paper as soon as the caller says it. I know that I am going to see it on my computer screen, but I want to make sure that if the name is different than what appears on my monitor that I have the correct name. If you have some other automated way of knowing the client's name, by all means use it, but be sure that you have that name ready for a quick reference anytime during the conversation.

Writing down the name may not be simple enough. Think back to Alicia and Marianne. If I were to answer the phone, I would write down A-leesh-a or My-anna and I might quickly ask them to spell it for me since it was an uncommon name.

When a call comes in and the name is difficult, I will alter the beginning of my conversation to bring attention to their name and to show the client that their name is important to me. Showing the attention to detail is a significant step in customer service and in most cases it makes an outstanding impression on the other party. It is not uncommon for me when asking a client's name to repeat it back and ask them if I am saying it correctly. For example I take a phone call:

Phil: "Hello this is Phil, can I please have your name?"
Caller: "This is Mr. Slombadowicz. (I immediately write down the phonetics as Slum-bahd-o-witch)"
Phil: "Wow, Mr. Slum-bahd-o-witch, I bet people butcher your name all the time?"
Caller: "You bet."
Phil: "I think I said it correctly. How close was I?"

Caller: *"You were close enough, don't worry about it."*
Phil: *"I do worry and your name is important, where did I
          go wrong?"*
Caller: *"It is Slawm-bahd-o-witch."*

The major difference here was how I pronounced
the beginning of his name, Slum vs. Slawm. The message
I have sent to Mr. Slombadowicz is that attention to
detail is important at Cooper. By taking the time to
insure the proper pronunciation of our caller's name,
we let him know we care about him. Saying a person's
name correctly is a small item that sends a powerful
message.

Rule 2: Use the name at least twice in the conversation

Once I have the correct name and I can insure that I
will pronounce it correctly, my next step is to use it at
least twice during the conversation. Using it twice is
actually quite simple, we use it in the beginning of the
conversation and then at the end. The beginning of the
conversation is actually very easy, once I get the name I
reply, "{name} how can I help you today?" The second
time I use the name is at the end of the conversation
during my summary and conclusion where I will say,
"{name}, is there anything else I can do for you today?"
It is just that simple. By using the name at the beginning
and end of the conversation, you have insured that it
has been used at least twice and you have once again
reaffirmed for the client that you know exactly who they
are.

Now I ask you to take a quick survey of how often
this simple step is followed. Over the next week as you
go to retail stores or make calls to people who do work
for you, see how often your name is said. Even more

interesting, call a Customer Service Department for one of the bills you pay. Of course, they are going to ask your name, but if you call five different companies, I will put money down that 3 of 5 will not say your name twice during the conversation. There are some companies that do on a consistent basis and it is not by mistake. Working with the representatives to insure they are using the name twice takes some work. Looking at this most simple of steps shows why WHAT + HOW takes practice and perseverance. Using the name twice is simple and then based on the length of the call we may need to say it more often.

Rule 3: Mix in the name sporadically throughout the conversation, but do not overuse the name

The number of times we use the name beyond the minimum of twice is based on the length of the call. There is a balance between not using the name enough and overusing it. I have looked for a ratio that I believe is sufficient in most situations. What I discovered is the use of the name every 90 seconds is within acceptable limits. This is not to say, at the 90 second mark, you should repeat the name, but rather use this as a guide to use the name the correct number of times, insuring that you do not over-use or under-use the name.

I have a tape of us calling the same leading computer manufacturer we looked at earlier in the discussion on the use of the word, they. This time, the customer service representative broke my rule with names. Do not overuse it. The call went like this:

Computer Rep: "Hi this is Andre, can I please have your name?"
Nancy: "Nancy."

Andre (the rep):	"Hi Nancy how can I help you?"
Nancy:	"I am trying to find out the status of an order."
Andre:	"Nancy can do you have the order number?"
Nancy:	"Yes I do, C129H79."
Andre:	"Thanks Nancy, give me a minute Nancy while I look that up for you (pause for 10 seconds). Nancy, I show that the laptop you have ordered was due to ship in one day. Nancy, does that give you the information you need?"
Nancy:	"Well, kind of. I cannot remember the method of shipping I requested."
Andre:	"Well, Nancy, I am showing that you requested standard ground shipping. Nancy would you prefer a different method?"
Nancy:	"Actually, yes, do you have second day available?"
Andre:	"Nancy, we do and I would be happy to make that change for you. Nancy would you like me to change the shipping to second day air?"
Nancy:	"Yes."
Andre:	"Nancy, I have altered the shipping to 2nd day air and your laptop will arrive in two days. Nancy, is there anything else I can do for you today?"
Nancy:	"No, that will be all."
Andre:	"Well, thank you for calling CustomersComeFirst Computer Company."

Andre used Nancy's name and 12 times and said it in about a 60-second span. This is actually a real life example and when I heard the tape I was shocked. I immediately went to work to determine why this was occurring. After a little bit of research about the customer service training program at this company, I found the training emphasized using the client's first name, but there was no mention of overuse. I'm certain, Andre was really pleased with himself as he accomplished what he set out to do. He did what he thought was correct, use the client's name, but he misinterpreted their meaning. I confirmed that this company never intended for Andre to use names as often as he was, but he had been doing this for over three months without any correction.

When you overuse the name it becomes forced and contrived and breaks our second rule of HOW, Customer Friendly. Remember, in customer friendly we want our conversation to simulate talking with friends or neighbors. I cannot remember ever speaking with friends or neighbors or witnessing a conversation where a person's name was used 12 times in just over a minute.

More appropriate would have been using the name in the beginning and the end with maybe one or two Nancy's sprinkled in if it felt appropriate. Reworking the conversation with this in mind we get:

Computer Rep: *"Hi, this is Andre, Can I please have your name?"*

Nancy: *"Nancy."*

Andre: *"Hi Nancy, how can I help you?"*

Nancy: *"I am trying to find out the status of an order."*

Andre: *"Do you have the order number?"*

Nancy: *"Yes I do, C129H79."*

Andre: *"Thanks. Give me a minute while I look that up for you (pause for 10 seconds). Nancy, I show that the laptop you have ordered was due to ship in one day. Does that give you the information you need?"*

Nancy: *"Well, kind of. I cannot remember the method of shipping I requested."*

Andre: *"Well, I am showing that you requested standard ground shipping. Would you prefer a different method?"*

Nancy: *"Actually, yes. Do you have second day available?"*

Andre: *"We do and I would be happy to make that change for you. Would you like me to change the shipping to second day air?"*

Nancy: *"Yes."*

Andre: *"All right. I have altered the shipping to second day air and your laptop will arrive in two days. Nancy, is there anything else I can do for you today?"*

Nancy: *"No, that will be all."*

Andre: *"Well, thank you for calling Customers Come First Computer Company."*

What a difference replacing the name with pronouns makes. In the second version of the call Nancy's name is only used three times and the conversation is flowing rather than being forced and not contrived. This is what we are attempting to achieve when we are using names and as a result we actually help to improve the 2nd step of HOW at the same time; the call becomes more Customer Friendly. Introducing the names into the conversation is important, but the question then arises, do we use the person's first or last name?

The use of first names versus last names

There are philosophical differences in determining whether the first name or last name of the other party should be used. Philosophy varies from company to company and from customer service expert to expert. Ultimately, I recommend whatever fits within into the culture of your company. Each school of thought has sound arguments, and therefore, I believe it is an organizational decision. Although my preference is the use of first names, I firmly believe the more important issue is using the name itself. My bottom line is that, although I have my own opinion, I always advise my clients follow the guidelines established by their organization and be consistent.

At Cooper Pest Control, Inc., I have borrowed the rules set forth by one of the guru's of customer service, Pat Croce. Pat Croce was the former President of the Philadelphia 76ers, a National Basketball Association team. He was also founder of a fitness enterprise. In the year 2000, he wrote a book in entitled," I Feel Great and You Will Too!" and I strongly recommend you adding it to your "must read" list. Chapter 10 is titled "The 10 Commandments of Customer Service" and Commandment Number Two is First Name Basis. At Cooper Pest Control, we follow the Croce Rules and Commandment Number Two In his book Croce says,

"Is there a lovelier sound in the whole wide world than the sound of your own first name being spoken aloud?

Of course not. Silk on satin is not nearly as smooth. A soft spring rain on parched ground is not as sweet or as welcomed. It is a basic vanity to which we are all susceptible. It is the first identity we learn. It is the first thing that separates us from everyone else. It is what we carry for our entire life.

So, at our Sports Physical Therapists centers (Croce was an entrepreneur superb, building an empire of physical therapy centers) we used a patient's first name, at every opportunity. Except when a person wished to be addressed by title—Doctor, Reverend, Father, Your Honor, etc.—or if he or she preferred the respect and formality of Miss or Mister.

Whatever pleased the patient pleased us".

I love the Croce rules and we live them, but I have added a few tips to making the rules easier to live by.

One of the questions I was asked early on in my WOW seminars was how do we know when to use the first name or Mister, Miss, Misses, Ms. There is a very simple rule that works very well. When the person you are speaking to, introduces themselves, the specific name they use will determine what we do next. If they use their first and last name, I take that as permission to use their first name. Say your first name and that is how I will address you. On the other hand if they introduce themselves as Mister Jones, I will reply back Mister Jones, even if I know his first name is Bill. Finally, if I know the person I am speaking to is a Doctor, Reverend, Father, Judge, I will always address them by title and let them specifically tell me to use their first name.

At Cooper, once we find out the person's name we need to find out their street address so we use this as our opportunity to ask for the address. So as a quick refresher and guide, here are the rules we use at Cooper for use of first names.

Example 1

Customer Service Representative: "Hello, can I please have your name?"
*Client: "My name is **Dr. Bill Jones.**"*
Customer Service Representative: "Dr. Jones can I please have your service address?"

Example 2

Customer Service Representative: "Hello, can I please have your name?"
*Client: "My name is **Bill Jones.**"*
Customer Service Representative: "Bill, can I please have your service address?"

Example 3

Customer Service Representative: "Hello, can I please have
your name?"
Client: *"My name is **Mr. Jones.**"*
Customer Service Representative: "Mr. Jones can I please have
your service address?"

It is really that simple and by following these rules, we subscribe to the Croce philosophy of the lovely sound of the first name while respecting those who wish to be addressed with respect. When I am returning a call to a client I will always begin with using Mr., Mrs., etc. and wait for the person to use their first name. Once they say their first name, which is most of the time, I switch over to a first name basis.

A question I am asked frequently is what to do if you are placing an outbound call to confirm an appointment, schedule a service or do some other customer related task and all you have is the name in the database. Unless you know the person and have spoken to them before and know their preference, you should also use Mr., Ms. If the database indicates that person you are calling is a Dr. or some other position of respect, you should use this instead. What should be avoided is Miss. or Mrs.

One of the greatest challenges I have found in the area of using first names is the use of Sir, Mam and Madam. The titles Sir, Mam and Madam are forbidden at Cooper Pest Control and this becomes a bit difficult when we hire someone with a military background. It becomes especially difficult if they just finished active duty or are in the reserves. Sir, Mam and Madam have been drilled into their heads and trying to break a new hire of this habit is quite difficult. The bottom line is that the habit must be broken. First names are a way of life at Cooper and if it takes perseverance and practice to make this happen, then practice and perseverance it will be.

Names are a powerful tool and when used effectively can add tremendous value to a conversation. By combining the proper use of pronouns and names steps 6 and 7 are rounded out making a nice set of soul mates leading us to our final set of soul mates, Ask Questions and Listen.

CHAPTER 14

HOW Steps 8 and 9—

Ask Questions And Listen

Ask Questions and Listen is the last pair of soul mates and the most powerful pair of items in What + How. When used effectively, Ask Questions and Listen provide the opportunity for the WOW moment. The other steps, Exude Confidence, Smile Factor, Pace and Enunciation, Pronouns and Names all allow us to deliver excellent customer service, the by-product of striving for WOW, but rarely do they provide us the opportunity to deliver a WOW moment. Remember the WOW definition?

WOW is achieved when the experience makes such an excellent impression with the receiving party that it is shared with family and friends. When striving for WOW, the by-product is an incredible experience, which impresses everyone with whom we come in contact with.

Using the tools and guidelines explored so far, help us achieve the by-product on a consistent basis. By asking questions and listening we will find the pots of gold, those WOW moments. For most people, asking questions and then listening are the hardest steps to master in How to Communicate. To become accomplished at this step a great deal of time, practice and role playing are necessary. Asking questions and then being disciplined enough to listen is extraordinarily difficult for people to do.

We all love to talk, especially when we know what we are talking about. When someone asks us a question, our first inclination is to answer them with the information we have. Instead we should stop and ask a question. By asking questions and listening we begin to understand what the other party wants, instead of making assumptions for them.

Asking questions and listening center around another step, Excellent Product Knowledge. It is very difficult to ask the right questions without having a fundamental understanding of the product or service we are representing. By taking this product knowledge and turning it into questions we set the stage for exploring for the WOW moment. If we are successful with our questions we will then be listening to the client the majority of the time, but this is where most customer service representatives fall down.

The 30/70 Rule

We all love to talk and this is the problem with most customer service. A good friend of mine has a saying, "With two ears and only one mouth, you should listen twice as much as you talk." I think he is being kind, I use the 30-70 rule; speak 30 percent of the time and listen 70 percent. Now, this is not possible in all situations but it is appropriate more often than not. The only way this rule works, is to ask questions and listen. When we are asking questions we are prompting the other party to respond, and as they do we gain knowledge. The best customer service professionals use this rule to their advantage to gain insight and find opportunities.

If you are using your two ears you will find the WOW opportunities and seize upon them. The only time you should be taking more is when you need to educate the client. If I am discussing a product they are unfamiliar with I may have to provide some background on the product so I can then follow-up with questions. However, a trap many fall into is once they start talking more at an appropriate point in the conversation, they forget to turn the talking off and keep on going. The mouth takes over and the ears stop working. The 30-70 rule will help you in your evaluation of your conversations, if you are speaking more than 30 percent of the time; chances are you have not asked enough questions.

There are three stories which really bring this point home. One is about Marriott, a leader in customer service, the second is a call I took at Cooper Pest Control and the third is a call we made to a leading retailer in search of shoes. All three show the power of asking questions and listening in finding WOW moments or in not finding the opportunity.

Marriott Ask Questions and Listen produce WOW

The Marriott story happened in 2000. My wife, Laura, and I were going on a business trip to Bermuda and were flying out of Philadelphia International Airport. One of my jobs is to make sure that all of our travel documents are in order, especially when flying out of the country. We arrived at Philadelphia International at around 8 am and we were at the ticket counter when the airline representative said, "Mr. Cooper, your documents are fine, but there is a problem with your wife's." "What is the problem," I quickly replied with a sense of wonderment and a lot of concern. "Well, Mr. Cooper you gave me your marriage certificate and that is not a valid means of identification, I need a birth certificate or a passport for your wife." Well, everything drained out of my body because I knew that what he had was all I had to give. I never checked our travel folder before I left the house.

I looked at Laura, and we quickly realized that she was not getting on the plane with me. I had to get on the plane to make the meeting I was attending and staying behind was not an option. I assured Laura I would do everything in my power to get her down to Bermuda as quickly as I could. I promptly called my office and spoke with my assistant Robin, who immediately went to work to rectify my error; while Laura left the airport distressed and in tears. I was not batting 1000 that morning. Over the next couple of hours, Robin was able to secure Laura's birth certificate and a new flight was arranged along with transport to the airport; this time, Newark, New Jersey. My mother, Sybil, agreed to take Laura to the airport.

Now the story gets interesting. The flight was scheduled to leave Newark at 12:30 from Newark. As 10:45 approached, my mother and Laura started the journey from Lawrenceville, N.J. to Newark Airport, about an hour's drive. Now there were things on their side. My mother is known for her lead foot, she was driving her six month old Lexus and they were headed for the NJ Turnpike. Laura was going to make this flight! The drive was going smoothly as they approached Newark airport, but the clock had just struck 11:50 and there was road construction. My mom realized the flight was due to take off in 40 minutes and she could not determine how to get to the departure gate. Now my mother is very bright and uses a great deal of common sense in her day-to-day dealings. This day, her choice would pay off. As she was in a state of panic, her eyes spotted a large building with a Marriott sign and on the side and she immediately headed toward it.

It was about 11:05 as she approached the bell stand and check-in area. One of the bell hops, Kodzo, approached the car.

Kodzo: Hello are you checking in today?
Sybil: Actually I need directions to the American Airlines terminal (with a bit of distress in her voice).
Kodzo: When does your flight leave?
Sybil: It leaves in about 35 minutes.
Kodzo: Well, I have two options. I can give you written directions to the terminal or I can hop in the back of the car and get you to the departure gate. Which would you prefer?
Sybil: Hop right in!
Kodzo: Just give me a minute I need to let my captain know that I am leaving the site.

Kodzo was back in just under a minute, got in the back seat of the car and they proceeded to the airport. I wish I were a fly on the wall, or fly in the car, over the next two minutes, because whatever conversation occurred between Kodzo and my mom, he gained the explicit trust of my mom.

As they pulled up to the departure area my mom stopped and turned around and said, "Would you mind coming up front and staying with the car? I would like to make sure my daughter-in-law is able to get on the flight." Now, you figure this is crazy enough just asking someone she met less than five minutes ago to do this. Add to the mixture that my mom was driving a brand new Lexus and she was in the metro New York area. This was simply a recipe for disaster. Instead, it was a recipe for WOW! The bellhop hopped into the front seat, and five minutes later when my mom came out of the ticketing area, there was the car and bellhop just where she left it.

A WOW moment!

What is really interesting is how this WOW moment could have so easily been an excellent customer service moment, but still have missed the WOW mark. Step back for a moment and let's review what occurred here and how the experience could have been so different. When Sybil approached the area near the bell stand a much different conversation could have taken place:

Kodzo: Hello are you checking in today?

Sybil: Actually I need directions to the American Airlines terminal (with a bit of distress in her voice).

Kodzo: I can certainly help you. Let me get the directions for you, we have them prep-printed and I just need to go to get them. Is that OK?

Sybil: Sure.

Now, let's look at the dynamics of the two scenarios. In the pretend scenario, Kodzo would have met Sybil's expectations and in fact would have had exceeded her expectations. When my mom asked for the directions, she was most likely expecting to get verbal instructions. Instead, a set of written instructions would have certainly exceeded her expectation. But would it have been a WOW moment? Definitely not.

Instead, what happened in the real life instance was Kodzo heard the distress in my mom's voice and proceeded to ask the $100,000 question, "When does your flight leave?" Followed by the million dollar question, "Well, there are two options. I can give you directions to the terminal or I can hop in the back of the car and get you to the departure area. Which would you prefer?" To ask the second question, Kodzo needed to have excellent product knowledge. He knew he had pre-printed directions that he could give her and he also knew it was OK to get in the car and help the lady in distress. Kodzo also knew that to deliver this service he needed to let someone know he was leaving the grounds and he knew who to notify. All of this leads to excellent product knowledge.

The two questions that Kodzo asked were simple, but in the process of asking them he uncovered a golden nugget, a WOW moment waiting to happen. Kodzo asked the questions and all suddenly realized the bases were loaded and he could hit a grand slam! It is really that simple. He asked the question and listened. I am certain that he must have sensed my mom's anxiety in her body language. And a WOW moment was delivered.

There is a funny footnote to the story that occurred while my mom and Laura were inside at the ticket counter while Kodzu was watching the Lexus. Once again the ticket counter would prove to be an interesting place on this day in May. Laura walked up to the American Airlines counter and handed over her ticket and the birth certificate. Everything should be in order, yes? Not quite.

American Attendant: Mrs. Cooper was your maiden name Weinstock?

Laura: *Why yes, how did you know?*

Attendant: *Well, this is your birth certificate with your maiden name and your reservations are in your married name. We will need a birth certificate with your married name or a marriage certificate.*

As luck or fate would have it, Laura had put her birth certificate in the same folder I had brought earlier in the day and remembered what started the whole ball rolling. Out came the marriage certificate much to the surprise and amazement of the American representative. Laura was not to be denied as she boarded the flight. The final chapter of the story with the marriage certificate made for fun story telling in Bermuda. A WOW moment and a twist of fate, it was a day I will always remember!

Thank goodness for asking questions and listening. Kudos to Marriott, for stressing customer service and teaching their people how to find WOW moments. Do I tell the story over and over? You bet! This is what WOW is all about.

Spotting Opportunity

In the summer of 2002, our phones at Cooper Pest Control were very busy and I hopped on a customer service line to lend a hand. At Cooper, we stress that everything is about serving the clients, and if that means you stop what you are doing to help, then that is what you do.

On this occasion I happened to take a call from one of out clients who was on a general home maintenance program. This service is designed to take care of a host of nuisance pests, including wasps. As the phone rang, I proceeded to answer:

Phil: *"Good morning this is Phil, can I please have your name?"*

Lucy: *"Yes this is Lucy Brown."*

Phil: *"Hi Lucy and can I have your street address?"*

Lucy: *"425 Stonepath Way, Princeton."*

Phil: *"Thank you Lucy how can I help you?"*

Lucy: *"Well, I am having a problem with wasps and I need to schedule a service call. I also want to let you know I am dissatisfied with the service as it does not seem your treatments are stopping the wasps."*

Now, at this moment I was listening intently and processing my WHAT knowledge. I knew Lucy's home service plan included wasps, but only when wasps had already built nests, what we call reactionary service. I also knew we had another program, Wasp Prevention that actually prevents wasps from building nests. With this in mind and bells and whistles going off in my head, I proceeded to ask questions to find out more information.

Phil: "Can I ask you a few questions?"

Lucy: "Of course, you can."

Phil: "When you first purchased your maintenance service with us what was the reason you decided on the service?"

Lucy: "Well, it was like I told you before, I need to stop the wasps at my house and my son is very allergic and I am very concerned with wasps and bees around my home."

Phil: "So, when you purchased the agreement you expected the service to stop the wasps before they became a problem?"

Lucy: "Well, isn't that what the program is?"

Phil: "Before I answer that I would like to ask you one other question. Are you concerned with any other pests like spiders, ground beetles, crickets, mice, and things like that?"

Lucy: "No, I really purchased the service to only to stop the wasps."

Phil: "Lucy, when we came to your home originally and sold you the service you currently have, did we discuss with you Wasp Prevention?"

Lucy: "No, but the program I have prevents wasps, doesn't it?"

Now I had all of my ammunition and understood that she was being provided the incorrect service. It was obvious that we had failed her in correctly identifying her original need. Opportunity was knocking for Wasp Prevention and we missed it. Even with this failure, I believe it is never too late to correct a mistake. You just have to own up to it, so I proceeded in this direction.

Phil: *"Well, I need to apologize for our guiding you to the wrong service when you originally signed up. The service you are in is specifically for general pests versus the wasp prevention which by the sounds of your answers is the program that should have been recommended for you. Before I describe these questions can I quickly set up a service call to take care of the current problem and can I also arrange to get you a quote on the other service?"*

Lucy: *"Yes you can."*

Over the next couple of minutes, I scheduled the service and then went on to explain how the service she had differed from the wasp prevention. When it was all said and done two days later, we cancelled her home maintenance agreement and started a wasp prevention service.

The call could have gone so differently if I had not stopped to ask the important questions. I can easily see a service call being set up for the wasps, and a customer who would continue to be frustrated by the apparent failure of the service being provided and ultimately a cancellation of service because a lack of perceived value. Ouch!!!!

Did I achieve a WOW moment? I do not think so. I am certain that Lucy did not rush to her family to discuss the conversation. But we did have an excellent by-product. We saved a client and provided Lucy with the proper service!

Was I happy about the fact that she was incorrectly sold from the beginning? No, I was not happy. Actually I was pretty upset. Even though we had erred in our judgment, there was a chance to correct it and that is exactly what we did. First, I gave her credit for all the money she had paid for the incorrect service we sold her. Then we looked internally to determine why this occurred in the first place. We worked with the representative who sold the account. When we sat down with our representative, it became very clear that he possessed all of the WHAT knowledge. So then, how did things go so wrong? My guess is the day our representative met with Lucy, the right questions were not asked or he was not listening. Just having the knowledge does not insure we are going to deliver the message clearly, and this has everything to do with how we communicate. Asking questions and listening can help us spot a WOW moment, and if we fail to ask questions and listen we can fail to meet the customer's expectations.

Paula, asking the right questions

Asking questions and listening helps us find opportunities for WOW moments, but when questions are not asked WOW moments slip away. I have a wonderful call that we made to a major retailer known for its outstanding customer service. Now before I begin, I can tell you I am a big fan of this company. Their level of customer service is typically superior and they really go out of their way to give you that WOW experience. I love shopping in their stores because of their superior customer service and attention to detail. A typical shopping trip to their well staffed stores is usually excellent one.

As with most, if not all organizations, bad moments occur and on this spring day in 2001, Paula, the representative in the shoe department, of this exceptional retailer, failed our test. The call to Paula is in my archives of calls we analyze in learning How to WOW our clients. I love to use this call as an example of questions that are not asked. The opportunity for a grand slam may have been present, the bases may have been loaded, the opportunity for a WOW moment present and Paula missed it for lack of asking questions.

I had one of my teammates Nancy call the local store looking for a pair of women's size five blue pumps. We picked this shoe style and size knowing that most shoe departments have a small selection of size five shoes and then add to it the specifics of blue pumps; we knew we had a recipe for an interesting phone call. So armed with her tape recorder, Nancy set off on a mission of finding her size five blue pumps.

The call went out to and Paula answered the phone. The conversation would last four minutes and 41 seconds and during this time Nancy was on hold for two minutes. Here is how the call went.

Paula: *Hi, this is Paula. How can I help you?*
Nancy: *Hi Paula. My name is Nancy. I'm looking around for a pair of blue pumps with a two inch heel. I wear a size five and the reason I am calling is I only have time to go to a couple of stores. It's just a really crazy time for me and I'm just calling around to a few stores just to see, ya know, what selection you have.*
Paula: *Um, OK, now I do have, [pause] you want navy right?*
Nancy: *Yes.*
Paula: *Navy blue, right? Um I have a pair, it's about two inches. It's Vaneli. The tip is patent. The shoe itself*

is a combination of patent and leather. Almost looks like leather dots. It's cute. And I do have another pair. But I'm not sure about your size. So could I ask you just to hold on for a minute and I'll check for you?

Nancy: Sure.

Paula: OK, Thank you.

(2 minute 15 second hold time)

Paula: Hello.

Nancy: Hello.

Paula: Hi, thank you for holding. I do have two pair.

Nancy: You do.

Paula: I'll describe them to you and I'll put them on hold for you.

Nancy: OK.

Paula: The first pair as I said before, it's a medium navy. In other words, it is not a real midnight blue navy. It's a definite navy though.

Nancy: OK.

Paula: The toe is patent. Um, the rest of the shoe is a combination of the leather and a very shiny leather, so it looks like almost patent leather dots on it.

Nancy: OK, how big are the dots?

Paula: Very small. I mean it's not an obtrusive or an obnoxious looking shoe. The other one is an all leather shoe. It's a very, very dark navy. It's like a midnight navy.

Nancy: OK.

Paula: That one has a stacked, wooden stacked, not a wooden, but a leather stacked heel . . . a rounded toe. And that's a calf, it's not the patent.

Nancy: OK.

Paula: And I have them both in a size five.

Nancy: You do?, OK. Do you usually have a large selection of five?

Paula: Well, we usually only get one size in. So once it's
            gone, it's gone. That's the problem. That's why I
            wanted to check to see if we still had any five's and
            yes we do.

Nancy: Ok, all right, let me think about it and I'll give you
            a shout back.

Paula: OK, my name is Paula. Um if I'm not here, I'm
            scheduled to go off the floor in a bit. So if I'm not
            here, you can just leave a message or you can give
            me a call back by . . . I'm just checking the time . . .
            by about 2:30, I should be back on the floor.

Nancy: OK, Great.

Paula: OK.

Nancy: Thanks a lot Paula.

Paula: You're welcome. Bye

Nancy: Bye.

On a very good note, Paula knew her shoes and
knew the stock that she had. In fact, I give Paula a very
high grade on her Product Knowledge. But Paula made
her first significant mistake at the 50-second mark. At
this point in the conversation, we established that they
had size five blue pumps, but Paula wanted to double
check on the stock and asked Nancy, "Is it OK if I put
you on hold for a minute?" Nancy's reply was "yes"
and then you hear nothing for two minutes. No music
on hold, nothing, just "white noise." It was not Paula's
fault that this store did not have music or information
on hold, but the bottom line was this was not part of
their phone system, at least which is what I think. I guess
Paula could have set the phone down. Instead, there
was nothing, but dead air time, and not for one minute,
but for two minutes and ten seconds. The time seems
like an eternity. When Paula asked, "Is it OK if I put
you on hold for a minute," the minute should have been
the standard. The last time I checked, a minute is 60

seconds not 130 seconds. The other thing Paula could have done was to advise Nancy that there would be just dead air, but not to be alarmed, she would be back to the phone in the time agreed upon. This is important because as you listen to the recording, you start to wonder at the one-minute mark if you are still connected or if the call was accidentally dropped. The lack of background noise, music etc. makes it difficult to know if your call is still active.

Remember, finding the WOW opportunity involves asking questions and listening and this is where Paula really falls down. During the conversation Paula does ask a number of questions, but unfortunately not enough. And most of the time spent on the conversation was Paula talking about her stock of shoes and what they looked like. Instead, Paula should have been asking questions and then intently listening to Nancy's answers and then following up the answers with more questions.

There are so many additional questions Paula could have asked. Take a moment and read the conversation again and then add in the questions below:

> *Nancy, when do you need the shoes by?*
> *Where do you live (perhaps there is another store nearby that Paula could have called to find other shoes)?*
> *What type of occasion are the shoes for?*
> *Do you already have the clothes that you will be wearing with the shoes?*
> *Can you describe the clothes you will be wearing with the shoes?*
> *Do you need any other accessories?*
> *Do you have a budget in mind for these shoes?*

Just think if we asked these questions, of all the possible answers Nancy could have provided. Imagine for a moment that Nancy had a very important affair to go to the next day, and money was not an object. Nancy called this store because in the past she received that outstanding customer service experience, and her bottom line was she needed shoes and needed them quickly. In fact, Nancy routinely drops $300-$500 for a pair of shoes and never blinks. On top of it, Nancy had recently purchased a new dress for the affair, but was not pleased with the accessories and was planning on shopping for them later in the day. Is this pretend situation possible? The answer is a resounding yes. This is the type of client this retailer caters to. The interesting part is, if this was the scenario, without asking additional questions Paula would have missed that WOW moment. Bases loaded, a grand slam opportunity staring her in the face on game day and she struck would have struck out.

Think of what else Paula could have done. She could have sent the shoes to Nancy overnight. Perhaps Paula could have called around to the other stores to see if they had other shoes in stock. Another possibility would have been to direct Nancy to the website to view the shoes. All of these possibilities could have led to a bases loaded opportunity, and a chance for a WOW.

Am I being rough on Paula? There is no question I am. Interestingly, I will play this call in the beginning of seminars and ask the participants to grade the call. Remember they have not been exposed to WHAT + HOW and Paula generally receives a six to seven on a one to ten grading scale. Inherently, most people sense some problems in the call, but it is still viewed as above average. By the time we get done with the seminar and review the 27 steps on the call, the grade comes sharply, down to a three in most cases and people are most critical of Paula is the Ask Questions and Listen section. The true customer service professionals master the skill of asking questions. Once we master this, and we listen effectively, WOW moments follow.

Listening

Developing excellent listening skills is critical to asking the right questions and listening. As the soul mate to asking questions, listening goes together like a horse and carriage or soup and sandwich! Once we ask a question we need to zipper our lips and listen intently to the response. Listening also involves observing body language if we are face-to-face with the client. Listen to the words, watch the body language and begin to formulate your next set of questions.

The key to listening is the amount of WHAT knowledge we possess, with an emphasis on Excellent Product Knowledge. Remember Step 1 of What to Communicate is Excellent Product Knowledge, and in order to listen effectively, we must possess this knowledge. If we are weak in our WHAT knowledge the first thing to suffer is the ability to listen to the caller.

Imagine you are a member of a call center and your WHAT knowledge is excellent. As is your teammates' knowledge. Your WHAT + HOW skills are awesome and you take significant pride in your ability to ask questions and listen. As you settle in to start your day, you turn on your computer and enter your call center software. Immediately you recognize there may be a problem as the software has a different look and feel. In about 30 seconds your phone will begin to ring as you are logged into taking calls. Quickly, you look over the software trying to understand the change and wonder how this change occurred without you knowing about it. Thirty seconds elapse, and the phone begins to ring. Of course, knowing the phone must be answered you do so while continuing to try and understand the software changes. Distracted, your listening skills immediately begin to suffer. This example is not all that unrealistic, as things change in our environment constantly. When things change, and we are not familiar with the change, our product knowledge decreases and our distraction level increases. With distraction comes a decrease in our ability to listen effectively which then affects our ability to ask questions and a viscous cycle is created.

To listen, your mind must be open and you must be paying attention. WHAT knowledge is key.

Listening is not Easy—Alice's Restaurant

A really fun and enlightening exercise I do in many seminars revolves around Arlo Guthrie's classic song, "Alice's Restaurant." I suggest you buy the CD, which is titled "Alice's Restaurant"; play the track "Alice's Restaurant" and do the exercise below. I have to give credit for this fantastic listening exercise to Patrick Quiqley. Quigs is President of Sales by Design and is a maniac when it comes to sales and sales seminars. He realizes listening is the key to finding nuggets of information. "With two ears and only one mouth, you should listen twice as much as you talk" is what Quigs says. I love listening to Patrick speak around the country and the energy he brings to sales forces. I always love to plug him for he is simply WOW!!! If you are ever in the market for a sales training consultant, this is your man. Check out his website www.salesbydesign.com to learn more about this remarkable trainer As a fan of Quigley I always remember him by the exercise he introduced me to, Alice's Restaurant. The exercise illustrates why people do not listen effectively.

To do the exercise, which I strongly recommend, listen to the first 11 minutes of the song. Yes, only the first 11 minutes. The song is actually 18 minutes and 34 seconds long. Below are a series of questions about the song. Do not review the questions before the song begins. Some of the questions have blank spaces. The object is to fill in all of the blank spaces and then fill in the answer to the completed question. Some of the questions are complete, in this instance all you have to do is fill in the answers.

Before you begin make a copy of the page with the blank spaces and unanswered questions (below). Don't worry, I will not turn you in for copyright infringement, you have my permission to make copies!

Do not cheat, go through the entire 11 minutes and see how well you do. The average person gets about five questions right out of 15. I have never had anyone go 15 for 15, even the people who know the song inside out. Try it and do not cheat, let the song play though the first time. On the next page you will find the answers. Once you have given it your best shot, look at the answers. Then I want you to play the song again and pull out a blank copy of the questions without the answers. Now see how you do and see how different the song feels.

Give it a try.

1. What is the song about? _____
2. How far from the railroad tracks is the _____ ?
3. Where does _____ live?
4. What is the _____ name?
5. What did the sign at the _____ say?
6. How big was the _____?
7. What was the _____ name?
8. What _____ and _____ did this occur in?
9. How many police cars and _____were there?
10. How many _____ x _____ were taken?
11. What was on the back of the _____?

12. What kind of _____ was in the _____?
13. How much was the _____?
14. What room was the _____ in?
15. What did the sign above the _____ say?

The Answers

1. What is the *song* about? Alice's Restaurant or The draft.
2. How far from the railroad tracks is the *restaurant*? One-Half mile.
3. Where does *Alice* live? Church bell tower.
4. What is the *dog's* name? Fasha.
5. What did the sign at the *city dump* say? Closed on Thanksgiving.
6. How big was the *cliff*? 15 feet.
7. What was the *officer's* name? Officer Obie.
8. What *city* and *state* did this occur in? Stockbridge, MA.
9. How many police cars and *police men* were there? 3 cars and 5 police men.
10. How many *8 x 10 color glossy photos* were taken? 27.
11. What was on the back of the *pictures*? Paragraph explaining what each one was to be used for as evidence.
12. What kind of *dog* was in the *courtroom*? Seeing eye.
13. How much was the *fine*? $50 (and pickup the garbage in the snow).
14. What room was the *psychiatrist* in? 604.
15. What did the sign on the *bench* say? Group W.

I have completed the Alice exercise at least one hundred times and I never cease to be amazed by it. Occasionally, when I am holding a seminar, I will get a real cocky group who is convinced they can get all of the questions correct or there will be someone in the audience who says they know the song inside out. When this occurs, I turn up the volume a bit to see how easy I can throw off their listening skills. I will walk over and start talking to the person next to them, or I will begin doing things to distract them like tapping on the desk. Of course, this never happens in real life when you are having a conversation. There are never disruptions or distractions. And the moon is made of Swiss cheese. Of course, there are distractions in our workplace and our ability to tune them out affects our ability to listen. More importantly, I believe it is management's responsibility to create the work environment that decreases the amount of distraction, so we can listen intently to what is being said. Just add a little distraction into the mix and without proper WHAT knowledge, the recipe for disaster has just increased 10 fold.

Now let's look once again to the Alice exercise. If you were lucky enough to do it, what you found is the second time while listening to the song, it sounded different. Your WHAT knowledge was so much better the second time around that you could concentrate on the song and the answers. In fact, I am certain you could be distracted a bit and still get most of it right and be able to ask questions. By increasing your WHAT Knowledge you can more effectively deal with the distractions around you.

Listening is one of the hardest things to do, but when you have the WHAT knowledge combined with effective listening and you use them both to ask questions, it is the stuff WOW moments are made of. "The nuggets are out there," as Quigs says, "you just have to find them!

Chapter 15

HOW Step 10—Avoid The Use Of Jargon

Avoiding the use of jargon will allow the other party to effectively listen. Conversely, when we use jargon, we force the other party to try and interpret what we are saying, and as a result, we confuse the other party. Jargon, as defined in the Merriam-Webster dictionary is,

"1. The technical terminology or characteristic idiom of a special activity or group.
2. Obscure and often pretentious language marked by circumlocutions and long words."

Jargon is used everyday and when we use it in customer service, the results can be disastrous. We must be on our guard not to use technical terminology that others do not understand and we must remember that jargon to one person is not jargon to another. This goes hand in hand with the definition that jargon is technical terminology of a special activity or group.

To avoid jargon, remember your first day in the industry that you are involved in. In my line of work, the pest control business, our world is filled with jargon. Clean outs, callbacks, crack and crevice, micro-injection, just to name a few. Now unless you are part of my industry, I doubt you can tell me what those items mean. We must always remember that the person who we are speaking with, is not always familiar with the words we use on a daily basis.

Jargon Changes Person to Person

What is one person's day-to-day language is another person's jargon. When one doctor is speaking to another doctor the words they are using, are generally different than when they are speaking with a patient. A good doctor knows to change the words being used so the patient can understand them. This is no different in our daily lives. For instance, if I am speaking to a commercial real estate professional and I use the acronym HVAC, the real estate professional immediately knows what I am talking about. My hunch is that only a small percentage of the people reading this book know what HVAC is, for those with curious minds it stands for Heating, Ventilation and Air Conditioning, which is the cooling and heating of the surrounding air. Therefore, it is important to know our audience when we are using jargon-type words. The tricky part is knowing what is jargon and what is not. Once again our ability to listen becomes important and if we are face-to-face with a person, we should be watching their body language. When we say a word the other party does not understand, they may look confused and we need to carefully try and determine what has confused them.

In the earlier example I mentioned that Cooper Pest Control performs clean outs and this is an excellent example of jargon. Imagine the following statement:

"Bill, we can do a mouse clean out for you or we can discuss a maintenance program, which would you prefer?"

Now, how is Bill to answer this? Are we sending a maid service to clean up the area, what is a mouse clean out? Now let's try this.

"Bill, we can do a one-time service for mice with a 90-day service plan. If mice return in the 90 days we will return at no additional charge. In addition we can discuss a maintenance program, that has broader pest coverage and continues well past 90 days. Which would you prefer?"

There is a significant difference in the meaning between the two scenarios and in the second example Bill will be able to make the appropriate choice. By simply removing the jargon and replacing it with meaningful words, Bill can listen and understand what is being said.

When speaking with the other party, pay close attention, if they sound confused. This is a pretty good indication that you have mixed in jargon that is confusing them. If you ever suspect this has occurred stop and ask the person you are speaking with if there is anything they did not understand or any words that are not clear. Remember, people are usually embarrassed to let you know they do not understand a word. They generally assume they are supposed to know what it means, and therefore will not let on that they do not know.

The Havahart Thing

In the pest management industry a widely used live trap for animals is made by the company, Havahart. One afternoon, I was checking out how my competition's customer service performance. I had Nancy call a large regional pest management firm to help her with a very unusual squirrel problem. Nancy pretended to be a potential client and told the customer service representative that she had squirrels running around in her backyard and she wanted them gone. Of course, there is nothing that can be done about squirrels running around the yard; this is just nature doing its thing. But, we were looking to see how the customer service representative responded to this silly request. Interestingly, during the call all sorts of jargon was used by the customer service representative. At one point she said,

> "They trap them in a Havahart thing and
> they take them some place else."

Now my question is, what is a, "Havahart thing," and "where is, someplace else?" Imagine if you were the client, the questions that would be running through your mind. Are we taking the squirrels to a pet cemetery? The connotations of "someplace else" are troubling at best. I am sure if the principles of this well respected company heard this conversation they would not be the least bit happy. Jargon can change the shape of the call and the perception of the client.

What happens when jargon is used

Another interesting phenomenon occurs when people do not understand words. Instead of asking for a clarification, the thought is to wait and eventually the meaning of the word will be clear. The problem with this is that the person is distracted and is not focused on listening to what you have to say or the questions you may be asking. Avoiding jargon is a very important part of HOW.

Jargon does not have to be words. It can also be phrases. Try this one on for size:

> "We begin our day at 7:30 and you can be
> our first stop."

So the question is, when will the person arrive at your house? By the words, you could make a valid assumption of 7:30. In fact, if a Cooper representative said this to you (and of course this would never happen) it would actually mean that our technicians start their day at 7:30 by reporting into the office or beginning their paperwork, and that we will arrive approximately at 8:15. What a difference! When 8:00 comes, and the client calls in, I can only imagine the phone call. The customer service representative would say up and down that they never told the client that we would arrive at 7:30. The client would be convinced that the stop was hard scheduled for 7:30. And because jargon was used, both are right. Jargon can be dangerous!

The only reliable way I have found to avoid the use of jargon is to have others not familiar with our industry listen to my tapes. I will ask them if there are any words I am using that they do not understand. The longer you are in an industry, or company, the more prone you are to using jargon. It is something you have to be acutely aware of, and always looking to correct.

CHAPTER 16

HOW Stelp II—Warm And Fuzzies

I view warm and fuzzies as the second major chance to WOW another person. The first chance was with Asking Questions and Listening. Warm and Fuzzies are the second. When we use warm and fuzzies effectively, we have the opportunity to create that WOW moment, the moment when the receiving party goes home and talks about what occurred to their family and friends. On the other hand, if warm and fuzzies are used ineffectively we can take the communication and just trounce it.

A warm and fuzzy is an adjective, anecdote or empathy and as much as I love warm and fuzzies, I also know how dangerous they can be, if you handle them incorrectly. I always remind new people to the WHAT + HOW system to work on warm and fuzzies after they have mastered most of the WOW components. Warm and fuzzies used incorrectly sound goofy and out of place, and take away from your message. The trick is to integrate warm and fuzzies over time. The best of the best in customer service use warm and fuzzies to their advantage to create those WOW moments.

I also view Warm and Fuzzies as a huge part of Problem Resolution. When we wrong a client, and we make the conscious effort to fix the problem, I call this problem resolution. Integrating warm and fuzzies into problem resolution, becomes a key factor in our success at turning the problem around. We will examine this closer in the Problem Resolution Chapter. The three steps to Warm and Fuzzies, adjectives, anecdotes and empathy are keys to the WOW moment and understanding what they are and how to use them become the key in WHAT + HOW.

Adjectives

Adjectives are very powerful things. Wonderful, fine, super, and marvelous. These are words that make the conversation come to life. If a bug is big or small it helps to describe what we are talking about. We can combine multiple steps when working with adjectives as we introduce inflection and tone, two parts of Pace. What we want to accomplish is to make the adjective to come to life with the meaning we intend, by adding inflection and tone to the word.

Anecdotes

Anecdotes are stories, and it is amazing what stories can do. The story does not need to be a novel, but it helps a person to understand what you are saying. Anecdotal reference to something brings a picture in the mind of the listener By painting a word picture for the other party, they begin to imagine what you are saying, and if you are a skilled storyteller, you can make quite the impression. When anecdotes are used effectively they are a very powerful tool.

Empathy

Empathy is particularly important when dealing with problem resolution. However, empathy must be sincere otherwise it will be perceived as patronizing. A great deal of the perception is based upon the tone you use. Throughout warm and fuzzies you will find that speed, inflection and tone impact the way the warm and fuzzy is received.

Warm and Fuzzies Meet WOW

In July of 2000, while on vacation, I was having dinner with my wife and we were about to experience one of those rare WOW moments. If you go to Palm Desert, California, stop into LG's Prime Steakhouse, and you will be treated to WOW service along with outstanding food. Alan Greenberg, the owner, had the best server I have ever encountered in over 40 years of dining. Although I have only had the pleasure of eating there once, Alan tells me each server is better than the next.

My wife Laura and I were out for a night on the town, and happened into the restaurant. It was a busy night at LG's. Pete, our server, came over to our table, introduced himself and quickly asked our names and where we were from. During the course of the next hour while we ate our meal, Pete would ask a question or two each time he came by the table to refill the water, while he was bringing our food or just checking in. There was no wasted motion. All of Pete's tables were filled, so he was not in the position to just chit chat, but by the time we came to dessert, he knew Laura and I on a personal basis. Pete was doing all of the things necessary to produce the by-product of WOW service, the outstanding consistent impression. He was just excellent, but we were not going home to speak about it to family and friends. Add to the mix that the food was outstanding, and we were very pleased with our choice. Then Pete turned on the Warm and Fuzzies and he accelerated into a different gear as he aimed for a WOW moment.

Pete: *"Phil and Laura, can I bring over the dessert tray?"*
Laura and Phil (almost simultaneously): [Chuckle with a smile.] *"Pete, we are so full there is no way we could possibly consider desert. When you get a chance you can bring over the check?"*
Pete: *"I apologize for letting you eat so much, I should have warned you earlier. Phil [pause], Laura, so you are sure to save some room the next time you come to visit, can I show you the dessert tray?"*

It was at this moment that I knew he was turning it up a notch.

Phil: *"Sure Pete. But I do not want to waste your time, there is not a chance that we could eat another thing."*
Pete: *"That's OK, it is not a waste of my time. I will be right back."*

About 30 seconds later Pete was back with his dessert cart with about eight items on it.

Pete: *"Now, Phil and Laura let me tell you about our first dessert (as he pointed to a tin with only one piece of pie in it). This is the last piece of Grandma's Apple Pie (I found out later that there is always one piece in the tin and it is always the last piece in the tin). Now this pie is made by a family in the mountains not far from here and the recipe is three generations old. It is baked fresh*

> *daily and we have it delivered once a day. You see this ice cream on top, well, it comes from McConnell's of Santa Barbara. Have you heard of McConnell's?"*
Phil: "No."
Pete: *"Well, McConnell's is known for their incredible ice cream and we only get our ice cream from them. They make the most incredible ice cream, using only the freshest ingredients, and it adds just the right touch to the apple pie."*

And Pete went on to do a story on each one. When Pete finished going through each one (in about two to three minutes total) he then said this,

Pete: *"Now Phil and Laura, you will be sure to save some room the next time you come?"*
Phil: *"I will and I want one of those."*
Laura: *"And I want one of those!"*

By examining what Pete did, Warm and Fuzzies can be completely understood. It is marvelous to watch a master of customer service at work with warm and fuzzies, and Pete is that master and he started with empathy. "I apologize for letting you eat so much, I should have warned you earlier. Phil [pause], Laura, so you are sure to save some room the next time you come, can I show you the desert tray?" The use of empathy, putting yourself into the other person's shoes is an effective tool. By using empathy Pete took away our defenses. What are you to say to Pete's first words? He accepted the blame for us eating too much. Now, this was one shrewd, savvy server, a skilled customer service professional.

Next, once Pete had our defenses down, he upped the ante by using anecdotes. Each dessert had its own story mixed in with a whole host of adjectives. Add a dash of questions, and the master chef of customer service created a WOW moment. Not only did we order the desserts, but we also talk about it to this day. This is what WOW is made of!

Whenever I think of Warm and Fuzzies, I think of Pete and that dinner. It was not by accident that Pete did what he did. He understands his craft, and the need to WOW his clients. Pete is the best server I have ever had.

The important thing to remember about warm and fuzzies is that they must be sincere and from the heart. Pete understands that, I understand that when I use them. If not used correctly, it can have disastrous results so be careful when using them. Practice the use of them and bring them along slowly. Warm and fuzzies are a great tool, but they must be used effectively. Imagine someone using empathy, but using incorrect tone and not sounding sincere? Or, imagine if Pete began telling stories about the desserts, but the stories lasted 10 minutes? What if we use the wrong adjectives to paint our picture? There are so many things that can go wrong when Warm and Fuzzies are used incorrectly that we must be sure of ourselves before tackling them.

CHAPTER 17

HOW Step 12—Summarize And Conclude

The final step in HOW TO COMMUNICATE is Summarize and Conclude. Step 12 seals the moment and allows us to have a consistent, excellent customer service experience. Every once in a while, it will produce a WOW moment, but more often than not it ensures we have not made any errors and supports the other steps, insuring that we always have an excellent by-product.

Summarize

When we summarize, we are doing a quality control check on our conversation. No matter how long I have been in customer service, or how well I think I have customer service down, I always remember that I am human and make mistakes. The summary allows me to catch major errors I have made during the conversation. By catching the errors, I prevent mistakes from happening in the delivery of the service.

When we summarize, we wrap up the important points of the conversation into one tight neat package. A quick example illustrates the point. In this conversation, I have set up a service call and have had a 90-second conversation with the client determining the problem and arranging a date for service. As we near the end of the call I say,

"Now John, we will be out to your house on Tuesday March 10 between ten and one. I have noted on your work order that you are seeing spiders in the first floor family room and you want us to check around your deck area for wasps."

What happens during the summary is very interesting. If I accidentally typed in the wrong day or time, John will correct me. Imagine for a moment, earlier in the conversation John and I agreed to a service time of 8 am to 11 am. As I typed it into my computer I accidentally typed "8 am-1 pm". During the summary John would hear me say:

"Now John, we will be out to your house on Tuesday March 10 between eight a.m. to one p.m."

There is a significant chance John will pick up on this mistake and correct me. This is one of the keys to summarizing. Of course, our objective is never to make errors, but it can happen and summarizing will help catch the mistakes.

Another reason for summarizing is the other party has a chance to tell us something they may have forgotten. Many times after a conversation we remember something else we wanted to say. By summarizing, we give the other party a chance to review in their mind what has been said, and many times it triggers other thoughts. For instance,

Phil: *"I have noted on your work order that you are seeing spiders in the first floor family room."*

John: *[John interrupts the conversation], "Can you also make a note that we are seeing about three spiders per day in the basemen?"*

Phil: *"I have added to the work order that in addition to the spiders in the first floor, you are also seeing them in the*

> *basement as well and are seeing about three per day. Additionally, you want us to check around your deck area for wasps."*

It is important to note, after the interruption, I did not repeat the entire summary. I repeated the spiders on the first floor as a lead in. It is amazing how many times the other person will interrupt you during the summary, and clarify or add something to what you already have.

The final reason for Summarizing is to show the client you have been paying attention. If we have used the 30/70 rule correctly we have been listening 70 percent of the time and we have been actively taking notes as part of Documentation. When we summarize it shows the client we have been listening to what they have been saying and we understand it. By doing this, you are saying to the customer, "You are important and what you said is important." Most conversations are not summarized and when this occurs the client is putting their faith into the customer service representative that they understand the salient points of the conversation. It is much better to build the trust of the client by showing them that you heard what they said.

The trick is to keep the summary concise and to the point. A long-winded summary is not what we are looking for. Instead, you should bring out the pertinent points of the conversation and keep it brief. A concise summary will do wonders for you and set the table for the final step, Conclude the Conversation.

Conclude

Concluding the call is simple, "[name], is there anything else I can do for you today?"

This simple ending has two significant effects. First, it insures that I have used the name for the second time. I always start my conclusion with the person's name.

The second effect is more profound. The conversation ends on the client's terms not yours. If we simply summarize and say, "thank you, have a great day" we would be ending the call on our terms. A quick review is in order by combining the summary and this incorrect conclusion:

"Now John, we will be out to your house on Tuesday March 10 between ten a.m. and one p.m. I have noted on your work order that you are seeing spiders in the first floor family room and you want us to check around your deck area for wasps. Thank you and have a great day."

After these words, the conversation ends, but it ended on my terms, when we want it to end on their terms. By changing the ending we can end the conversation on their terms.

"Now John, we will be out to your house on Tuesday March 10 between ten and one. I have noted on your work order that you are seeing spiders in the first floor family room and you want us to check around your deck area for wasps. John, is there anything else I can do for you today?"

The other party has one of two choices at this moment. They can either answer "No" or they can say "Yes" and then proceed to tell us about something else they would like us to know. In either case, it is not us ending the call, it is the other party. Eventually, the client will answer the question with a "No" and we can then complete the call by saying, "thank you and have a great day" or whatever other parting line you would like to use.

I find it fascinating what happens when we ask the question, "Is there anything else I can do for you today?" If someone is calling Cooper Pest Control to schedule a regular maintenance service and we ask, "Is there anything else I can do for you today?," rarely do they respond with yes. There is a basic reason for this. When they are calling for a maintenance service they are looking to get on and off the phone. Their objective is simple, find a time that Cooper Pest Control can come to their home that is convenient for them. So typically, after we summarize the appointment and ask our concluding question, the answer back is, "No."

Interestingly, there are many calls we receive at Cooper where the answer to the question, "Is there anything else I can do for you today?" is a resounding "YES." The most common time this occurs is when we are working with new clients. We have spent a great deal of time asking questions and listening, drawing from the client what is important. However, once we summarize, the major points of the conversation, the client gets a chance to hear what we perceived were the important discussion points. So many times when we conclude under these circumstances, the new client turns around and says, "YES," to the question, "Is there anything else I can do for you?" It is simply because they have so much they want to say, and more often than not, it does not all come out in the first round of questions.

When this occurs there are new opportunities for additional questions and listening new opportunities to WOW the client. The conclusion is so very important, especially when the other party has not said everything that is important to them.

Concluding multiple times

If I conclude and the client says, "Yes, there is something else," and a new topic comes up then the next logical question is, "Do I summarize and conclude all over again?" Only summarize the new points, or any changes the other party has made to previous points. And yes, you must conclude again with, "Is there anything else I can do for you today?" If you summarize all of the points a second time, you will sound like a broken record. The first time, the customer affirmed what was correct or incorrect in our summary. There is no need to do it a second time.

Instead, what we want to summarize are the important points of the new information. Just as in the first summary, we need to insure our information is correct and we will again conclude with "Is there anything else I can do for you today?"

Every once in a while, the other person will throw you a curve ball by answering the question by saying yes more than once. Imagine you have already asked "Is there anything else I can do for you today," twice and both times the answer has been "yes." Now, you get to the conclusion for the third time, and you need to conclude again, but you do not want to sound like a broken record. It is at this point I put a little humor at the process and I would say something along the lines of:

"John, I know I have already asked you twice is there anything I can do for you today, and both times you came up with something. I want to let you know I cannot end this call without asking that question. So I can be sure I have all the bases covered. Is there anything else I can do for you today, John?"

By inserting some humor we take the edge of the question and lighten the moment. It certainly is customer friendly and still achieves our goal of always concluding the conversation on the other party's terms.

So remember to always summarize and conclude and keep on doing it until the other party gives you permission to end the call.

CHAPTER 18

The 10 Objectives of Customer Service

Now that we have the five steps of WHAT combined with the 12 steps of HOW we are set to begin to master the 10 Objectives of Customer Service. The 10 Objectives are the questions we ask ourselves when the conversation is complete to see how well we did overall. The WHAT + HOW steps help us practice the skills. The 10 Objectives help us understand whether we struck out, hit a single, a double, a triple, a home run or hit that magical Grand Slam, the WOW moment.

The objectives are the things we see and hear in customer service speeches and books, and although they do not form the basis for practice, understanding them and answering them cannot be ignored. There is a reason they are so widely written about, you can practice all you want, but if you do not achieve the objectives then you ultimately fail the client. The 10 Objectives are very simple and determine our ultimate success or failure.

#1 Did you WOW the client?

WOW is our first objective. It is really that simple, did we WOW the client? WOWing the client is the basis for this book, the basis for the WHAT + HOW system and everything we strive for. This is where we determine if we believe the client if going to speak about us later today in a positive manner or if we achieved the by-product. Remember, we are consistently shooting for the WOW moment, but looking to achieve the by-product of WOW, a consistent, outstanding customer service impression. When I go back and listen to a conversation, if I realize there were opportunities for a WOW moment, and if I missed them, I will lower my score. The objective is to WOW the client.

#2 Did you Increase level of customer satisfaction?

We are always looking to increase, the satisfaction of our clients, with our products and/or services. It is so important because, if we have satisfied customers, we will increase the level of customer loyalty. Conversely, if we ask this question, and cannot effectively answer it with a yes, then we probably did nothing to increase their satisfaction with us. In a world where competition is striving to steal our clients, we must always answer this question with a resounding yes. Notice, I use the phrase "steal our clients." Actually, when we do not increase the level of customer satisfaction, our competition does not steal anything, rather we lose our clients. The ball is in our court to keep our clients and by increasing customer satisfaction, our chances of increasing customer loyalty increases dramatically.

#3 Did you insure that our client wants to use us now and in the future?

Number three also goes hand in hand with customer retention, but it is slightly different than number two.

We need to sit back and ask ourselves if we were the client, would we be inspired enough to only want to use us? If the answer is yes, then we have succeeded in this step. If we cannot answer this question, then to some degree, we have failed in meeting this objective.

#4 Does the client perceive value in working with us?

Number four is a tough one to evaluate, but I believe we should always be asking the question of ourselves. I am always working with my team in the understanding of the value concept, as it relates to the people who do business with us. The question of value places your product or service against the multitude of choices your client has. We all make value choices every day and in order to retain the loyalty of clients they must perceive value in what we provide to them.

Perception of value as it relates to client retention at Cooper Pest Control is a cornerstone of what we do day-to-day. Client retention is far more important than bringing on new clients and it is our number one priority. The basis for retaining clients is insuring they perceive value in working with us. Our competition is not just other pest management firms, but it is all of the other things our clients can do with their money.

The majority of our clients do not have to use a pest management service. This is especially true in the residential marketplace. Our client has contracted with us to either protect their property, health or simply because their tolerance for pests is low. The trick is to show the value of the service we are rendering, to build the customer loyalty.

Occasionally, we will get a call from a client wishing to discontinue their service because they are cutting back on their budget. There was a time when we would simply accept this answer with the knowledge they could no longer afford our service. This is no longer the case, as we know when our client says they are canceling to reduce expenses what they are really saying is, "I have chosen to cancel your service so I could afford to do other things that bring greater value to me." When we get a cancellation due to budgetary reasons, it is indicative of a general failure within the company to show the value of our service. By the time the customer is canceling, it is in most cases way too late to correct the problem.

At every turn in customer service, we must be asking ourselves, "Does the client perceive value in our service?" Asking this question must be part of every conversation we have and that is why I include it as objective number four By forcing ourselves to ask this question, we are helping to insure the client retention that is so important in the success of our organizations. If we complete a conversation and we cannot answer this question clearly, then we have left the door open to all of the other products and services seeking to replace us in the client's value equation.

#5 Do you understand the client's needs?

Number five is wrapped around our HOW steps of asking questions and listening. If we were effective in asking questions and listening, then there is a very good chance we understand the client's needs. Understanding the needs of the client is critical to our ultimate goal of superior customer service. When we explored asking questions and listening, I provided the example of Lucy Brown and Cooper Pest Control's error in not asking the right questions. To quickly recap the conversation, Lucy called about a problem with wasps. After listening, I recognized that she was in a service called Home Intensive that was incorrect for her need of preventing wasps. Instead, the correct service Cooper offers is Wasp Prevention. By asking questions and listening, I was able to quickly determine Lucy's primary need, an effective service designed to prevent wasps from building nests on her house, so her son who was allergic to stings would be less likely to encounter wasps. We can take this a step further by recognizing that the original Cooper representative who went to Lucy's house failed on step number four. Our representative never understood Lucy's needs, and sold her a service, our Home Intensive service, in which she could never see value.

When we have excellent product knowledge and we combine it with intelligent questions, and intently listen, we can insure we understand our client's needs.

#6 Did you determine the most appropriate products/services based on their needs?

Our sixth objective builds on number five by processing the information we have gathered concerning our client's needs, and then evaluating our products and services to determine the most appropriate. It is very important to remember that our clients do not know all of their options. This objective integrates a variety of WHAT + HOW Steps: WHAT number one, Excellent Product Knowledge, WHAT number three, Clear Presentation of the Options, HOW number seven and eight Ask Questions and Listen. By integrating these, we can evaluate all of the options available, and then guide the conversation toward those that are best suited to the client. As we guide the client in the direction we believe to be correct, it is very important we continue to ask questions and listen, to insure that our decision making is correct.

Putting all of this together, takes a great deal of practice. When we listen to tapes, and practice, it is always interesting to go back and carefully ask if we determined what was the most appropriate product or service. When we are asking this question to ourselves, we need to be critical about the questions we have asked, and if we truly know the client's needs.

For example, let's look at a simple call that involves scheduling the visit of a service person to my house. I call into the company and wish to schedule the appointment and the call goes something like this:

Phil:	*"Hello, this is Phil Cooper. I would like to schedule the maintenance for my air conditioner."*
AC Company:	*"I would be glad to help you Phil. Can I please have your phone number so I can bring up your account?"*
Phil:	*"999-555-1212."*
AC Company:	*"OK Phil, I have your account. We are scheduling appointments for next week. Do you have a preference between a morning or afternoon?"*
Phil:	*"Afternoon would be fine."*
AC Company:	*"I can schedule our technician to come to your house between 12 noon to 5 p.m. Does that work in your schedule?"*
Phil:	*"I (hesitation) guess that would be fine."*

Now, at this point, the representative is listening intently and hears the hesitation in my voice as well as the verbal cue "guess," and looks to determine the best product/service for the client. In this case, the product/service is actually the time his company will come to my house.

AC Company:	*"Phil, I sensed a hesitation in your voice, would you prefer a narrower time frame?"*

Phil:	"That would be great, I cannot sit around all afternoon waiting for your person to arrive."
AC Company:	"I have one of two options for you. Our first option is that we can narrow the time frame down to a two-hour window. Let's say for example 12 noon to 2 p.m. Our other option is for you to call in the morning of service, and we can tell you within one hour of our arrival time. Do you have a preference?"
Phil:	"I would prefer the two-hour window."

Now as I am requesting the two-hour window the customer service representative is looking at their schedule for next week and is looking specifically for open appointments in the afternoon and for two-hour openings. As he looks, he sees that Monday and Wednesday are very busy, but they are going to be on my street on Tuesday and the best time is from 1 p.m. to 3 p.m. He has determined the most appropriate service based on the client's needs. In addition he has used his product knowledge of the schedule and combined this with the questions to the client along with the responses to come up with an option for next Tuesday that fits both the client's needs and achieves efficiency for the company.

AC Company:	"How is next Tuesday between 1-3 p.m.?"
Phil:	"That would be great."
AC Company:	"OK. So, to quickly review, we will be to your house next Tuesday between one and three p.m. to perform your spring maintenance on your air conditioner. Phil, is there anything else I can do for you today?"
Phil:	"No, I am set."
AC Company:	"Well, you have a great day [conversation ends]."

These same concepts continue whether we are on the phone or face-to-face with the other party. Insuring we have determined the most appropriate product or service based on the client's needs, allows us to continue on to the next objective, Insuring the Client Understands the Options.

#7 Does our client understand their options?

Once we have presented the options to the client we have to insure that the client understands the options and although it is similar to number five and number six it is different and unique. In objective five, we determined the client's needs and in objective six we provided the most appropriate products and services based on those needs. In objective seven, we are insuring that the client understands the options available to them now and we are determining if there are other options the client should be aware of for the future.

Objective seven insures that WHAT number three, Clearly Present the Options, was handled correctly. Is this a bit redundant? To me the answer is yes, it is redundant, but a necessary redundancy. We can clearly communicate the options to the client, but insuring that they clearly understand them, is a different matter.

I have found that this is one of the areas where many customer service representatives have difficulty understanding the significance of this step and fail. The difficulty begins with the belief that once we explain something to someone, they are expected to understand it. Have you ever been involved in a situation where two parties are not on the same page and during the conversation one of the parties says, "But I told him . . ." The failure here is in the word "told," which is a one-way communication. It is critical that once we explain the options, we insure the other party clearly understands them.

The trick in understanding options is using our HOW techniques to achieve the desired result. We once again are asking questions and listening. If there are multiple options, and we have explained them, we might ask questions that position the options versus what we understand the client's needs to be.

In the summer of 2003, I received a call from a client who was confused and upset with services we had provided. The end result was that our client never understood the options. This client was particularly upset because they had read an article in the *New York Times* on my brother and his revolutionary methods in Carpenter Ant Control and they were also familiar with our WOW mission. The expectations of the client were high and that rightfully so. However, things went terribly wrong. We failed to live up to the minimum expectations, and we clearly failed in insuring the client understood their options.

How this occurred is a classic example of what can go wrong in a communication process and why looking at this objective separately is so important. Our business developer, or what others call sales representatives, met with the client and dropped the ball during this visit. Our client started the conversation by informing our representative that their reason for calling was they were seeing carpenter ants and were concerned about protecting their investment. Right away, our client established one of their needs as the protection of their investment; the buildings on their property. The buildings were the main house, the garage, the barn and the study. Our representative then looked at the carpenter ant problem, provided estimates for each of the structures and discussed the options for the carpenter ant services our company offers. The client signed the agreement to have the services rendered and our representative left happy with the result.

The euphoria of a good sale wore off as I became involved. Our technician, Bob Walker, went out to the home and immediately knew the customer did not understand their options, and began trying to correct the error. It is never too late to correct errors, and Bob knew he had work to do. The most pressing item was that, in Bob's opinion, the barn and the garage actually did not need carpenter ant control and he proceeded to discuss this with the client. The outcome was that we only treated the house and the study thereby reducing the price accordingly. Bob called to give me a heads up, and before I could call the client, they were on the phone asking to speak with me. I had a wonderful conversation with the client as she re-hashed what had occurred. I asked a couple of questions as the conversation centered on the two buildings for which we gave estimates, which really did not need the service. The client was concerned why our sales representative misled her into believing all of the structures needed a treatment. This is an unacceptable practice at Cooper Pest Control, and I spent a great deal of time working through this issue with this particular representative.

As the discussion continued, what became obvious was that other very important options were not understood by the client. Remember the client wanted to protect their investment and a big part of this was protecting against termites. The option for proactively looking for termites, a service called TermAware, was never presented to the client. Therefore, at the initial meeting two mistakes were made, the option of not treating two buildings were not discussed and the option of incorporating TermAware, into the program was brought up.

Where this becomes the classic example, is the interpretation of the events by our business developer. This was a new representative with the company, and although he had been through WOW training, he made this classic error. I sat down with my representative and asked him to explain what occurred. His response was, "But I explained all of this to the client." I replied, "And how did you know that the client understood his options?" Where he quickly answered, "I asked them if they had any questions about what I had said, and the answer was no."

Our representative failed by asking a yes-no question, instead of an open ended question. He was so intent on explaining the programs and providing estimates that he failed to ask questions that would help determine if the client truly knew what he was explaining. Some of the questions that he might have asked were:

"Mrs. Jones, between the two programs, TermAware and the Cooper Carpenter Ant System, which do you feel best protects your investment?"

"Mrs. Jones, although I am recommending only treating the two structures, do you see a need for treating the other two structures?" If a yes/no answer were given I would immediately respond with a polite, "Can you please explain why?"

The bottom line is that we need to be sure once we have explained the options; the client truly understands what we have said. Without doing this, we will never know if they actually were able to comprehend what we were speaking about and our ability to WOW the client can never occur. We can discuss the options until we are blue in the face, but unless the other party understands what we are speaking, about it really does not matter. The bottom line is simple; does the client understand his/her options?

#8 Does our client know the various products and services we offer?

I believe an educated client is the best client, but we need to be careful not to be perceived as constantly pedaling products and services. Although similar to "clearly presenting the options" it is different in the aspect there are many products and services we may offer which may not be options at the moment. Imagine trying to explain all of the potential products and services during each communication. As a result this objective is tricky, especially if we have a multitude of products and services. Balancing too much information with educating our clients is a tightrope we must walk.

A good habit to get into is asking the other party one simple question about a product or service they may not be familiar. Remember that products and services also include other methods of doing business with our firm. For example, the client may have been able to use our website to obtain the same information as was obtained on a phone call, but they may not realize it. Perhaps we recently introduced a new service and we are getting out the word on it.

I include this objective to remind ourselves to keep our clients informed. It may not happen on every communication, but it should occur during most conversations. By keeping it in the front of our minds, we will continue to make the concerted effort to continually educate our clients.

Whenever I am having a conversation with a client I have a list of other services we offer. I will choose one to ask if they are knowledgeable about it or if they have interest in learning more about it.

#9 Did you find opportunities to increase value, business opportunities, sales, and level of customer satisfaction?

Finding opportunities is key to WHAT + HOW and finding those opportunities will increase your chance for the WOW moment. Number nine is a simple question we must ask ourselves if we spot opportunities. The answer to this question helps me understand if the type of questions I am asking is achieving the desired result. If my answer to this question is "no," then I must step back, analyze the conversation and determine what different questions I could have asked.

If we answer "yes," all of the time to the question, "Did we find opportunities to increase value, business opportunities, sales, and level of customer satisfaction," then it is important to ask yourself, "what did you or the client do with the opportunity?" As part of the WOW process, we listen and grade our phone calls and in my workshops with company's customer service representatives we will ask this question. A common occurrence is the quick response of "yes" to this question, but when we explore how we are sure of this, the result is not so clear. We must be watchful to analyze this one carefully.

Earlier in the book we explored a conversation with a leading retailer where Nancy was looking for size five blue pumps. When I use this example in seminars the crowd goes wild, especially those keen retail shoppers. Paula, the shoe department representative, did not spot the opportunities to increase value and sales.

A quick review of the conversation and what occurred will bring the point home. Nancy calls looking for size five blue pumps and Paula describes two shoes she has available and offers to put them on hold for Nancy. What Paula fails to do is ask questions to Nancy in search of opportunities. Seeking these opportunities is the essence of this objective. Some of the questions that could have been asked would have been,

> ➤ *"Nancy, when do you need the shoes by?*
> ➤ *Where do you live (perhaps there is another store nearby that Paula could have called to find other shoes)?*
> ➤ *What type of occasion are the shoes for?*
> ➤ *Do you already have the clothes that you will be wearing with the shoes?*
> ➤ *Can you describe the clothes you will be wearing with the shoes?*
> ➤ *Do you need any other accessories?*
> ➤ *Do you have a budget in mind for these shoes?*

Each of these questions was filled with opportunity and had she asked Nancy the questions the WOW moment was staring Paula in the face. Opportunities were present throughout the conversation, but it required Paula to do some searching to find them. Nancy was not going to volunteer the information, and when Paula did not ask questions the opportunities were lost forever.

Finding the opportunities is a special skill that needs to be developed. When we are continually working on it, we will improve our ability to spot the opportunities. This does not mean that we all need to become salespeople, but it does mean that as an exceptional customer service representative we need to be make every effort to find opportunities to increase value, business opportunities, sales and the level of customer satisfaction.

#10 Did you develop client's trust in you?

The WOW system is complete with something that I place right next to WOW and that is TRUST. The words, "I trust you" carry great weight. Once you put your trust in someone, you expect them to uphold this trust. As part of the WOW system, we want to continually build the trust of those we come in contact with. As we build the level of trust, greater customer satisfaction, loyalty and our chances to find the WOW moment will increase.

The lifeblood of customer service, like our daily lives, is based on building the trust of others, and trust forms the backbone for superior customer service. Trust also brings with it customer loyalty, and in many cases the chance to correct our mistakes. If we have worked diligently on building the trust of our client, and we make a mistake and try to correct it, there is a greater chance that the client will work with us in correcting the problem.

Trust is earned over time and can be lost in a blink of an eye. We must always be working to build and refresh the trust of our client and we must always remember how easy it is to lose this most sacred, valuable item.

CHAPTER 19

Ready, Set, Go.

Putting WHAT + HOW into Action

The basis for the WHAT + HOW system was creating a system we can practice to place us on the same level as other professionals. Now it is time to take the five WHAT steps, the 12 HOW steps and the ten Objectives and put them into action. How we practice, how we grade, and how we make this part of our daily routine is what I consider the backbone to the WOW system. If you read this book and do not practice the things we have explored earlier, you stand a tremendous chance of just being another average customer service representative. This chapter is in many respects the most important part of this entire book. Join the professional athletes, The New York Philharmonic, stage actors and all other professionals who pursue excellence through practice of great skills. Implementing the WOW system gives us this opportunity to take customer service to an entirely different level. Raise the bar, and become the best you can be!

Why Practice?

When looking back at the current state of customer service it is easy to understand why customer service professionals fall down so often. Their organizations do not instill the belief that practice is necessary. This was the problem we faced in 1997 at Cooper Pest Control. Our team was providing above average customer service, but was not providing WOW service. Once I had developed the WOW system the next step was giving the team tools they could use to practice. Enter the tape recorder and grading sheets. We record conversations once per week and grade them to improve our performance and that also includes me. It is amazing when I take a week off of taping myself, I will begin to form bad habits once again.

Practice is not for everyone, and customer service is not for everyone. At Cooper, we have had our share of ups and downs in finding the right people who want to WOW our clients. It was not easy finding the people who were dedicated to this process. You have to want to be a professional, and do the things necessary to become one.

At Commerce Bank, headquartered in New Jersey, they have a saying, "It is one thing to believe in WOW, it is another to live WOW. Do you have the Guts to WOW?" The bank has realized not everyone is cut out to deliver WOW service, and they speak of guts. It does take guts to want to WOW clients. There is a level of dedication and you have to be willing to do things others will not. The same guts are necessary when you tape yourself. No one likes listening to their conversations and grading them. Even worse is giving your tape to someone else to listen to. It takes guts to do this and without the guts we will never achieve excellence. I hear many excuses when I travel the country as to why taping does not occur. Before we look at how to grade let's first explore why people never take the step of taping themselves.

Excuse One, I cannot stand listening to myself

Very few people like to listen to themselves on tape. When I speak around the country, the hardest thing to instill in the companies I visit is the ongoing taping and grading. It is so easy to say we are going to do it, and then a week goes by, then months and before you know it we are back to being average communicators.

You must make the commitment to excellence and this begins with taping your conversations once per week and grading them. You must incorporate this into your schedule and make it a priority. When you tape yourself, the important thing to remember is that, you are grading yourself. This is not about your supervisor checking your calls for quality assurance; it is about improving and practicing YOUR skills. You will need to take time to go through each of the WHAT + HOW steps and critically analyze the conversation.

Once you start the process and you begin to improve, the tapes do not sound dreadful. There is some consolation in knowing that all of your peers feel the same way about listening to themselves.

Excuse Two, There is no time to grade

I often find that for one or two weeks new people exposed to WOW will tape themselves, and then they fall into the trap of not finding the time to grade the tape. Once grading stops then the next step is to eliminate taping. Taping and grading are individual and organizational commitments that must be taken seriously. However, it must be viewed as an investment because it does involve a great deal of time, and it must provide a return on investment. The return on investment is achieved when we are hitting high marks on the ten objectives of WOW.

A two minute conversation takes approximately 20 minutes to grade if we are evaluating all of the items in the WOW system. Part of the system is grading ourselves, and then giving the tape to a teammate to cross grade. On average, this is a 40-minute investment per week and it must pay off for it to become part of our daily routine. In a job market where greater and greater demands are being put on us, where does this time come from? The answer is simple. There must be an organizational commitment, and recognition of the importance of the practicing the steps necessary to WOW. With the commitment, we must carve out time in our schedules on a routine basis to tape, grade and then cross grade. If we make the excuse there is no time to grade and practice, then our ability to WOW will be severely hindered.

In 2003, I started working with The Gale Company, a real estate firm committed to delivering WOW service. They are working hard to make the commitment necessary to achieve the WOW moments. During my preparation for working with the Gale team, I was having a planning session with their management team. During the meeting, I was exploring their culture and the things they do to drive their point home. Hung on the wall was a poster titled, "Our Way," which detailed two ways of thinking; "Their Way" and "Our Way." I inquired about the origins of "Our Way" and although it is not a Gale original, it was "Gale-Themed" by Trish Therault and Erik Slettleland of The Gale Comapny.

I have reprinted Gale's, "Our Way" in the appendix of the book and I encourage you to take a look at it. The poster has two columns. The first is "Their Way" and the second is "Our Way". In the Their Way column are all of the common excuses for failure to achieve and the "Our Way" shows how it is turned into a positive.

"Not enough time," is in the "Their Way" column followed by "We'll reevaluate some priorities," in the "Our Way" side. It is so appropriate when we speak about taping, grading and practicing; it is easy to say we do not have enough time, but it is a commitment to reevaluating the priorities to practice and grade that will turn you into a customer service professional.

I challenge you to re-evaluate your priorities to make practice a way of life for yourself.

Grading Sheets

The system is not complete without the grading sheet you will use to grade yours calls. In the back of the book, you will find a blank grading sheet. You can visit my website, *www.whatplushow.com,* and download a grading sheet. You are permitted to use this grading sheet and may reproduce it in accordance with the restrictions provided in copyright notice on the first page of this book.

On the grading sheet you will find all five What to Communicate Items, the 12 steps of How to Communicate and the 10 Objectives of WOW Customer Service. Knowing how to use the sheet is fundamental in being able to practice. Each item gets a score based on a one to 10 scale. A score of one indicates a total failure on the item and 10 is a perfect score. If you score 10s across the board, on the WHAT + HOW areas, then the Objectives must follow with 10s. And if you score a 10 that equates into a WOW moment and you must be sure the other party is speaking about you around the dinner table in a positive fashion; the definition of the WOW moment.

Getting people to be honest with themselves is very important and this is the reason for the cross-grade. When I first start working with people new to the system, I find some people grade themselves too high or too low. By having others cross grade your conversations you will get a better assessment of how others view your ability to WOW. This will help you refine your grading of yourself.

Tape Yourself, Grade Yourself

The commitment you must make to achieve excellence is to tape yourself once per week and then grade the conversation. The conversation only needs to be two to three minutes in length. If your conversations do not last two minutes, you may decide to do more than one. If your conversation is longer than three minutes, then pick a portion of the call not to exceed five minutes and grade that portion. Of course, you can listen and grade more; you will only get better and better. You only need to grade three to five minutes of the phone call. Try and find a call that is of this length or shorter. If all of your calls are longer, then you may need to listen to parts of the conversation or know that it may take much longer than 20 minutes to grade the call. If you are taping conversations in the field, pick parts of communication and grade them. Listen to the beginning of the conversation, the end and some in the middle. From time to time, listen to an entire conversation.

Once you have the conversation taped, your next step is to grade it. Remember as mentioned earlier, grading is more difficult than it sounds. So let's explore how to go about grading your conversations. I recommend as you begin grading you follow the system I have outlined below, but once you get into the flow of grading you are encouraged to switch the flow of things around,. Just be sure to grade all of the items.

How To Grade, Step by Step

Step 1   Listen to the entire conversation, or the parts you plan on grading, once. Do not stop the tape. Just listen to the entire conversation once through, to get an overall feel of the conversation.

Step 2   With your Tips for Grading at your side, pick one of the HOW steps and play the conversation a second time from the beginning. When picking a step to grade I like to start with HOW first and then come back to the WHAT section. Additionally, I recommend not starting with Exuding Confidence, since that encompasses our ability to master the entire system. Before starting the tape look at the tips for grading for this specific item and remember each tip is part of the overall grade for the step. Start the tape and concentrate on the step you have picked and the questions surrounding the step. Try not to think about the other items, maintain your focus on one item. Focusing on one item at a time is very difficult to do when you first begin grading yourselves. When I am in workshops, we will play three to four conversations before the participants begin to adapt to breaking the conversation into its smallest components. Work hard at maintaining your focus, and remember to focus on the item you are grading. Even this focus, you will hear things that are related to other steps, when you do, just jot a note next to the step with your comment. For example, if we are grading Asking Questions and we recognize that poor product information was given, you should stop the tape, and make a note on the grading sheet next to Excellent Product Knowledge. You will refer to this note when you eventually focus on Product Knowledge. Once you complete the note, start the tape again and re-focus on the step you are grading, in this case Ask Questions.

Step 3   Grade each of the remaining HOW items, but do each one at a time. The only exception is when you reach the soul mates. Remember they are each distinct, but the pairs are linked at the hip so they do affect each other. As you move from one item to the next, remember to replay the conversation as many times as you need. When you first start grading, be sure to play the conversation over and over to insure that you are focusing on the specific item you are grading. An example of this would be what to think about when grading Customer Friendly. As we listen to the tape we should be asking, "Did the conversation have rhythm?" "Was it like speaking to your neighbors?" "Did you do anything that was particularly friendly during the conversation, and were there unfriendlies in the conversation?"

When I give seminars, I will grade a call with the group for the first time. So often I will ask if the call was Customer Friendly and at least 50 percent of the group will give it a grade of six or seven. Then, I will start to ask questions to make them think a bit more, and we will play it back again. You should see the surprised faces in the crowd and moments later the score is adjusted downward. Be critical of yourself, but come up with reasons for your grade. On the grading sheet you will see an area to the far right for comments. This is where you should write your justification for your grade. If you run out of room continue writing on another sheet of paper.

Step 5   Grade the WHAT section, one item at a time.
Step 6   Finally move to the Objectives and grade them one at a time.

WOW, you are finally finished! You will be amazed at how different the call sounds when you listen to it each time. The time invested into grading effectively will now pay off as you practice.

Items Scored Best Through Cross Grading

There are some items that are best scored by the Cross Grader. Product Knowledge, Clear Presentation of the Options and Ask Questions are the most common ones needing cross grading. The Objectives are the other place where cross grading is critical since they tie all of the steps together. I find when we grade these steps on our own, we may give ourselves a higher grade than we should. This occurs because each of these steps is tied to product knowledge and our grade is based on what we understand about the product. The only way to know if our questions were on the mark based on our product knowledge is to have someone cross-grade and evaluate our product knowledge, options and questions. Perhaps, there was information we did not convey to the client and it is because we were not aware the option existed. If we do not know about the option, how can we communicate it? If we cannot communicate it, we will not consider it during our grading.

The three items, Product Knowledge, Presentation of the Options and Ask Questions, all require knowledge of your product or service, and it is very difficult to determine how educated you are. When I am working with other companies and their customer service teams, I rely on their people to help me grade the conversations in these three areas. When you are grading these areas, you might even let a few people listen to the conversation for their opinion on how well you conveyed your product knowledge.

Vary the person doing your cross-grading. By getting differing opinions on your conversations you will gain other insights to help improve. Remember, this is not an exact science and people will grade differently. There are many times when I am grading with others that we have disagreements over certain items, and we will discuss the point for a lengthy time. What is important is that everyone is thinking about the point and is evaluating what they heard. It is the same as all other professionals, there are multiple ways to be the best, and cross-grading will help you find the other paths.

How to Practice

It is easy to say that you should practice, but where do you begin? Based on my experiences with, the myriad of customer service professionals I have worked with I, advise everyone to pick the one item that they think they can score a ten on the quickest. Focus on that step and only that step. As you go about your day and you are speaking with people, try to remember the item you are working on and focus on becoming better at that item. It is very important that you do your best not to "practice" with your clients. Role play, if you can, with your teammates. This is preferred, but many of us do not have the additional time to do this consistently. Instead, by focusing on that one item, at a time and becoming skilled at that item we are able to improve without decreasing the quality of the call. On the other hand, if we try to work on more than one item at a time, the likelihood of getting confused, and botching the call increase. You do not have to grade all 27 items on each call you grade. Instead, focus on one aspect of WHAT + HOW and work to improve that step.

Once you have had a number of repetitions practicing the step you have chosen, ask yourself, without listening to a taped conversation, what your grade might be? If you believe you are scoring around an eight on the item, verify your conclusion by taping a call and then grading the one particular item. This will not take 20 minutes, rather you may only have to listen to the call once or twice so the length of this grading session will between five and seven minutes. Once you score between eight and 10 on a taped conversation, give the tape to a teammate and let them cross-grade you only on that one item. This will help conserve time as you refine your skills. Keep doing this for all of the 27 steps of WHAT + HOW. As you master an item, move onto the next one in order of difficulty. Your order of difficulty may be very different from your teammates. Commonly, it takes an above average customer service representative four to six weeks to score consistently 8-10 on all aspects of WHAT + HOW. It is not easy, which is why practice is so important.

During this period of ramping up, you should also do a complete grading once per week. Tape one conversation and grade on all of the items to see how you are progressing overall, and give this to a teammate to cross grade. It is important to avoid bias in your assessment of yourself, cross grading helps in this aspect. The commitment to grading is an important one and will take time. It is a habit you will need to form and you need to make the commitment to yourself. Remember, most things in life come with a price and in this case it is the determination to continue grading and improving.

Tips for Grading

As you begin to grade yourself, the following are some quick tips to consider when grading each of the items; you will find a copy of this in the appendix section, Quick Grading Reference.

WHAT To Communicate

Excellent Product Knowledge

- Did your statements match up with company collateral regarding the product/or service you were speaking about?
- Did you remember all of the important items about the product?
- Were there things about the product that you should have been discussed in the conversation?
- Were you clear in your descriptions of the product?
- Was there any other product knowledge that could have prompted other questions/
- Were you able to integrate any other technology (computer etc) without affecting the call?
- Be sure to have this area cross graded to insure that your knowledge of the product was appropriate.

Communication of Expectations

- Does the client know what to expect?

Clear presentation of the options

- Were too many options presented?
- Were any options presented?
- Did the client understand the options being given?
- Be sure to have this area cross graded to insure you presented the proper options.

Only communicate what is needed to make a decision

- Was anything communicated that posed an issue where one did not exist?

Documentation

- Did you find opportunities to provide items in writing to the client?
- Did you document the call well with well written notes for others to refer to?

HOW to Communicate

Exude Confidence

- Was confidence oozing out of you?
- Did you hide behind policies or company procedure (bad confidence/black sticky tar)?

Customer Friendly

- Was the conversation like speaking with a neighbor?

- Did the call have a rhythm to it?
- Were their any unfriendlies in the conversation (unauthorized hold, excessive hold, patronizing the other party, etc.)?
- What Customer Friendly things did you do?

Smile Factor

- Were you smiling during the conversation?
- Did you use body language during the communication that was positive in nature?

Pace

- How was the beginning of the conversation, a neutral pace is important to show that you are not rushed, good speed, inflection and tone to create positive first impression
- Was the speed of the conversation at a speed which the listener could understand?
- Did the speed of the words have a rhythm, at times faster at times slower?
- Did you inflect on the words bringing them to life?
- Did you use tone that was positive in nature?

Enunciation

- Could the other party clearly understand what you were saying?

Pronouns

- Did you avoid the use of four letter word of customer service, THEY?
- Did you emphasize I, we, us, and you?
- Did you reference teammate's names or department names?

Names

- Did you follow the rules of your organization as it relates to the use of first vs. last names?
- Did you pronounce the name correctly throughout the conversation?
- Did you say the name at the beginning of the conversation?
- Did you say the name at the end of the conversation?
- If the call was more than 90 seconds, did you use the 90 second rule and mix in the name additional times?
- Did you overuse the name during the conversation?

Ask Questions

- Did you ask questions during the conversation?
- Did you employ the 30/70 rule? (if you spoke more than 30 percent of the time, you probably did not ask enough questions)?
- Have someone cross grade this for you to see if there were opportunities for other questions that you did not raise.

Listen

- Did you employ the 30/70 rule and listen 70 percent of the time?
- Did you hear everything the client said?
- Did you have to re-ask any information due to not hearing the client correctly the first time?

Avoid the Use of Jargon

- Were any words used that the receiving party did not understand?

- Did the receiving party become confused at any point during the conversation?

Warm and Fuzzies

- Did you use adjectives?
- Did you use anecdotes?
- Did you use empathy?
- If you used adjectives, anecdotes or empathy was the client's reaction positive?

Summarize and Conclude

- Was a precise summary provided at the end of the conversation highlighting the major points of the communication?
- Did you conclude with, "{name} is there anything else I can do for you today?"

Keep the Bar High

At Cooper Pest Control, I insist, that we keep the bar high on our grading. The only way to improve is to have high standards. Keeping the bar high can at times be a challenge. The natural inclination of most people is to want believe they are doing a good job, resulting in a bar that is not rising. The challenge is to motivate your team while raising the bar.

It is critical when a new hire begins that they know the bar is set high. You can accomplish this by grading a few tapes with the new hire and allowing them to see how you would grade the tape. You can also watch them grade the tape to see if they are consistent with the company's standards.

Another interesting time to check on the bar is during cross-grading. This is one reason that from time-to-time I listen to tapes from everyone in the organization. What I am looking for is the grade our representative gave themselves as well as how the cross-grader evaluated the tape. It then provides a tool for coaching. If I think the bar is too low we will sit as a group and listen to the tape so we can raise the bar back to its proper level.

Striving to achieve our WOW mission at Cooper Pest Control is not an easy task. Perseverance and hard work in maintaining a high bar allow us to reach WOW everyday.

The Tools of the Trade— Your tape recorder

Although you can use whatever equipment you desire, I strongly recommend a voice activated cassette recorder. Through trial and error I have become a staunch supporter of the Radio Shack recorder. It is voice activated which I view as very helpful when taping conversations. It hooks up to any phone system and works just fine. There are also an increasing number of phone systems that will allow you to digitally record your conversations.

However you record the calls, the customer service representative should be in control of the recording device. The WHAT + HOW system is designed to be a self-help system and by keeping the recording device in the hands of the customer service professional, we are empowering them to improve.

At the end of the book, I have included an appendix on how to set up the Radio Shack equipment with almost any type of phone. This information is also contained on the *www.whatplushow.com* website. If the model of the recorder changes or instructions change, I will do my best to have the most current information about the recording equipment online.

The Tools of the Trade—Headsets

I am a firm believer that if you utilize a headset, your ability to document the conversation increases dramatically. Therefore, as I work with organizations, I am always hopeful that they will integrate headsets into their daily routine. At Cooper, we utilize cordless headsets to give us maximum flexibility. I have found that Hello Direct is a superior company in providing a variety of headsets to fulfill the need. Take a peek at their website *http://www.hellodirect.com* and consider utilizing a headset, if you do not already. For your reference, in the appendix I also show a setup with a tape recorder and the headset. It includes diagrams to make the process easier for you as you venture into the land of recording with a headset.

Taping and the Law—Over the Phone

Whenever you are taping it is important to insure you are complying with state and federal laws regarding the taping of conversations. In addition, to the items contained in this book, you should check your state's laws and always double check to make sure the federal and state laws have not changed in reference to this topic.

For years, I misunderstood the laws regarding taping and how the federal law and most state laws interpret the taping of calls. From 1997 to 2003, at Cooper Pest Control we always would start the conversation by saying, "This call is being monitored to insure WOW customer service." It turns out, that in New Jersey, this was not necessary at all. There was no need to advise the client that the call was being recorded. Let me explain.

The Federal Law is straight forward, as long as one party of the conversation consents to the call being recorded, then it is perfectly fine to record the conversation without advising the other party. The important part here is one party must consent.

In the WHAT + HOW system I strongly recommend that the customer service representatives record themselves with a tape recorder at their desk. I am a believer in self improvement and if the representative is in control of the tape deck, success of the self-improvement program is more likely.

Since the tape deck is controlled by the representative that is the consent that is needed. Therefore, it is not necessary to advise the other party that the call is being taped.

If the recording is controlled away from the desk, the phone system is doing the recording, and the customer service representative does not consent to the call, then it may be necessary to advise the client that the call is being recorded.

It is important to check your state laws to see if there are any laws or regulations that are more stringent than the Federal standard. Also, check to insure the federal or state standards have not changed.

Taping and the Law—Face-to-Face

If your staff is interacting with the public face-to-face I still recommend taping themselves. This book is not simply about phone customer service, it is much broader than that and it includes all face-to-face customer service representatives. Whether we are in the service industry delivering a service to a home or business or we are in retail, the WHAT + HOW system still applies. As a result we need to record, listen and grade, just as we would if we were speaking on the phone.

What you should do when you record a conversation as a matter of law, and what I believe is appropriate is different. As of the writing of this book, there are no Federal Laws that prohibit the action of recording face-to-face conversations. Additionally, you do not have to advise anyone that the conversation is being recorded. However, my recommendation is that you discuss what you are doing with your client. At Cooper, we started introducing taping to our technicians in late 2002. It is an interesting process putting the recorders into the field and the perception of our clients.

The process we follow is, when we arrive at the client, we ask their permission to tape while doing service. We do this for a couple of reasons. First, we are wearing a clip on mike so the client can visually see the recording device. Second, if the tape recorder drops out of the technician's pocket or something goes wrong it is not an embarrassing situation.

After we ask for permission, the client responds one of three ways. They answer, "yes, no, or why?" Rarely do we get a straight yes. More common is the why or no answer. The idea of recording throws people off, and the natural inclination is to think we are up to something no good.

If the client asks WHY, we provide a quick explanation of the WOW process and how by taping ourselves we can grade the conversation and the 27 items, so that we can improve our skills in the effort to deliver WOW customer service. You should see the reaction that follows from the client. They have never witnessed anything like this and are simply amazed and impressed. The really neat thing is that in most cases, we have an instant WOW moment as the client is so taken back by our commitment to customer service. Once we have answered why we are recording, rarely do we receive a negative response from these clients. Rather, the client is intrigued, and usually asks follow-up questions regarding the process.

If the client says "no", this is my favorite part. We take the recorder out of our pocket along with the mike and hand it over to the client and ask them to keep it until the service is over. This actually is the last thing the client expects us to do and in most instances the WHY questions follow. Once we answer the WHY questions, the client almost always hands back the recorder and gives their permission to proceed with the recording.

The impact we make on the customer during this process is simply amazing. They love the fact we take communication so seriously and go to the lengths of self improvement. The result, many of our clients discuss over dinner the wacky customer service company that wanted to record themselves to get better. This is another WOW moment!

Making Practice Fun — Rottler Pest Control

Making practice fun takes WOW to another level and I have to take my hat off to Rottler Pest Control for achieving this. In the winter of 2003, I had the good fortune of visiting Rottler Pest Control in St. Louis, Missouri. Rottler is a family run business owned and operated by two brothers, Mike and Gary Rottler. Together they have developed a company that strives for WOW customer service everyday.

What is most impressive about this organization is the time invested into role playing on a weekly basis. Each week they have team meetings and these meetings have been ongoing for years at Rottler. The meetings are ingrained as part of the Rottler culture. When the sales staff and technicians gather for this meeting not only do they discuss the events of the week, but they role play to improve their interactive skills. Even before I started working with the company, Rottler had made the time investment to strive for superior customer service.

Once I left Rottler, they integrated the WOW system into their role playing, and now they add the grading to their role playing on a regular basis. As I travel the country, I look for organizations that have made this commitment to role playing. It is rare when I find one as committed as Rottler. Kudos to the Rottlers.

As excited as I was, what was more fascinating was what occurred while I worked with this organization. During the seminar, they realized that although they were role playing with their sales and service people, they had ignored the customer service team as part of the role playing experience. This changed after I left and they added their customer service team to the role playing exercises. Next, Rottler added the WHAT + HOW grading system and to their routine. Now, they role play, and they grade their role playing. What a really neat way of practicing!

Finally, with all of this really terrific stuff came my favorite. Two days after I left, the Rottler team was hard at work role playing. Intrigued by the WOW process Dennis Vogelsang, one of their supervisors decided to add a twist to their role playing. Next to an interior door separating two work spaces he mounted a door bell along with a full length mirror along side the door. Then they began role playing. One by one, they would have a person on each side of the door; one person acting as the customer, the other the Rottler Pest Control technician. On this day, they were practicing one aspect of WOW, The Smile Factor! How much better does it get than that!

According to Dennis, the first time they did the exercise the pressure on the participants was tremendous. However, they repeated the exercise a couple of weeks later and everyone had made adjustments and the results were remarkable. A positive WOW experience for all! Rottler is an organization that takes customer service to heart, and wears it on their sleeves. This is what WOW is about.

CHAPTER 20

Tapes And The Pulse Of The Organization

As part of the commitment to WOW customer service at Cooper Pest Control, I continually listen to the tapes of our people. I can never listen to enough conversations. I believe listening to tapes enables executives of the company to find areas for strategic improvement.

I find two types of tapes most interesting. The first is a tape of our new teammates early in their development with Cooper Pest. The second is listening to seasoned veterans of the company, as well as managers. Each brings a different perspective to the pulse of the organization.

New Hires

As an organization, I do not want to make excuses for a new member of the team. It is always important to remember that our clients expect the same level of customer service from a new hire as a 20-year veteran. As a result, learning the WOW system and taping early in the development of a new hire is critical at Cooper. Taping sets the tone for what is to be expected in their conversations with our clients and our teammates.

Understanding the basic principles of WHAT + HOW and integrating them into their days becomes essential. When we hire someone new, within their first three days they go through basic WOW training, a one and a half course that lays outlines the principles of the system.

At week three, we have a four-hour WOW class where they learn how to grade conversations. This is the launching point for ongoing taping and training. This is also my chance to get a pulse on the organization.

Keeping the pulse through new hires is such a valuable experience. It affords you an opportunity to observe the training process, the impact managers and supervisors are making on the new hire and the attitude of the new hire. When Cooper Pest hires, we look for attitude. We always know we can train the skills, but the person must have the WOW attitude and the guts to WOW. When I listen to the tapes, I begin to obtain insight into all of these things.

New hire tapes also help establish new initiatives within the organization. We are able to spot new opportunities for new products, better training, better aids, and enhancements to our software, and the list goes on. There are times when we have recently introduced a new service offering and it is through the tapes that we recognize areas of confusion in our staff. We work very hard to make sure everything is crystal clear, but when the questions begin coming from our clients to a new hire, the holes in our internal communication become apparent.

When I think of new hires, I think of Andre in our Customer Service Department and how we did a poor job of explaining our one-hour window process to him. Through the tapes we were able to see a hole in our training and avert a problem. Andre misinterpreted the

WHAT knowledge he had gained and by listening to the tapes we were able to help him correct the error.

Accident Tapes

For years I have been cross-grading tapes of our staff and to this day I continue to get what I call accident tapes. These are the conversations I am listening to while I am driving and I hear something so wrong that it could almost make me lose control of my vehicle. I do maintain control of the vehicle, but I can promise you that it is nerve wracking to listen to this kind of tape.

The important thing is that I continue to listen and help my staff to improve. In fact, while listening to the tapes, I am able to spot weaknesses in our organization. Maybe we have provided poor product knowledge, or the tools we are giving our teammates are inadequate. Whatever the case, the tapes help identify areas where the organization can self improve.

Keeping The Pulse

I view listening to the tapes as keeping a pulse on the organization and the various departments. It is a great management tool to see how our staff is performing and where we can improve. This is especially true with a new hire. The beauty of a new hire is that they will make mistakes that show the weaknesses of the organization clearly. I love listening to the tapes of new hires to help gauge our overall training and the baseline level of customer service. The organizations expectation is to WOW our clients and that begins with every person in our organization, including our new hires.

After all of the years of taping and grading you would think I would get used to listening to tapes of new hires and the errors they make. As our training improves so do the tapes, but I still avoid listening to them in the car!

CHAPTER 21

Problem Resolution

"To Err is Human, To Recover is Divine" is the essence of problem resolution. Problem resolution is the art of taking a problem and turning it around. The ultimate objective is to turn the problem into a WOW moment. The best customer service companies know how to take problems and turn them into opportunities.

The first time I first heard the saying, "To Err is Human, To Recover is Divine," was during a training session I observed with Commerce Bank. The trainer, John Manning, was giving the Commerce Traditions class, a full day of WOW, which is given to every Commerce employee when they are hired. Commerce instills, in their people, the belief you must WOW everyone all of the time. However, they recognize the basic fact is, we are all human and we make errors. It is the acknowledgement of the statement, "To Err is Human" and turning it into WOW by seeking that divine moment that makes the saying so powerful. I agree with Commerce totally, there is no better feeling than recovering from a problem. The chance to deliver that WOW moment, to take that upset client from the being angry to being WOWed, it is the best natural high we can achieve in customer service. To fully achieve problem resolution and deliver the WOW moment you need to be ready for game day and have the WOW system working with a specific emphasis on a few WOW steps.

Acknowledge and Apologize

In the winter of 2003, I had the great fortune to listen to June Van Klaveren, an excellent customer service consultant out of St. Louis, Missouri, provide a talk on problem resolution. June has some unique perspectives on customer service and specifically on problem resolution.

The formula June advocates centers around three important actions that a company can take when dealing with customer problems. Listen, Apologize or Acknowledge and Fix. I was riveted to her talk as she laid out a very nice neat package on dealing with unhappy clients. What intrigued me the most was the concept of apologizing or acknowledging? In the Van Klaveren model you need to analyze why the customer is upset and then either apologize or acknowledge the error. The key is not to apologize when you should be acknowledging the error. When we acknowledge a problem, we must empathize with the client to begin the problem resolution. Take a look at June's website *http://www.compelcom.com* and *http://www.TheEdgeUp.com*. She does some really neat stuff and it is worth taking a look at.

WOW and Problem Resolution

All of the steps of WHAT + HOW are involved when we get involved in a problem resolution call. However, there are specific steps which we emphasize. We begin with warm and fuzzies and then turn on asking questions and listening, sprinkle in pace, coupled with outstanding product knowledge and we have the ingredients for a divine recovery.

As President of Cooper Pest Control, I want to hear from any client who is not WOWed by our service. I make it extremely easy for clients to be able to reach me by having my e-mail and phone number with extension on as much marketing material as I can. Every one of our service orders has a statement from me that explains our WOW process. The objective is to encourage our clients to let me know about their experiences, both good and bad. I am fortunate to get many notes and calls from clients who have had a WOW experience, but additionally, I do receive calls where Cooper Pest has committed an error. When the dissatisfied client call comes in, I heighten my senses with only one goal in mind, WOW the client. I aim to make them into the most satisfied client we have by the time I finish.

The call always begins with Warm and Fuzzies and I start with empathy. How empathy is used will make or break the call. Empathy is such a powerful tool when it is used effectively, but if it is not sincere or it sounds forced and contrived, the result will be disastrous. To begin with, we have a client who is already upset, and if we sound hokey, condescending or simply sound like we are just giving them lip service, it will just aggravate the already upset client. When I use empathy, I am going to put myself completely in the shoes of the client and express how upsetting the situation is, and how severely it has strayed from our WOW process. I want to insure the customer knows it is completely acceptable for them to be angry, and it is OK for them to vent as much steam as they want. As I tell them it is OK to be angry, I am using tone and inflection to emphasis the words "OK." It is critical for the client to truly believe that if I were in their shoes, that I would be hopping mad.

At this point, in most conversations, the client begins to explain what occurred. Most of the time, as the story unfolds; they get on a roll and get more upset as they go. Letting the client vent is very important, and my listening skills must be sharp. Additionally, I am typing away as I take notes of everything they are saying. Documenting their side of the situation is critical, especially as I try to come up with solutions. We will also use the detailed documentation internally, as we determine where things went wrong within our systems to create the client dissatisfaction.

Coming back to June Van Klaveren, it is after the venting of the client that acknowledge or apologize take center stage. We need to determine whether to acknowledge or apologize and it is important to choose the correct tactic. According to June, if the problem is NOT the company's fault, you acknowledge the error. If the problem is the customer's fault or beyond your control, you also acknowledge. You only apologize when it is the company's fault. Here are a few examples

Example 1

Client: *I've been transferred several times; I think you people just want to waste my time.*

This is the company's fault, therefore we apologize.

Company: *I understand why you are upset and if I were in your shoes I would be furious. Can I help you? Afterward I will find out what happened.*

Example 2

Client: *I just spoke to an older women who made me feel stupid, when I told him about my problem with the jeweled dog collar I ordered.*

This is the company's fault, therefore we apologize.

Company: *I'm sorry you were treated this way. No one should be made to feel stupid. I am upset you feel this way and will look into it after we complete our conversation. Can you tell me about the problem?*

Example 3

Client: *Well, I just assumed if I was not satisfied with the service your company would refund my money. Nobody told me that you didn't.*

In this example the company does not have a money back guarantee, and it is completely out of your control. You are also not in a position to refund the money although you think this is the proper thing to do. As a result, you need to acknowledge the misunderstanding and search for a resolution by asking a question.

Company: *I'm sorry for the misunderstanding; we don't have a money back guarantee. What parts of the service are you not satisfied with?*

The trick with all of these is to be sincere and the proper use of pace (remember pace is made up of speed, inflection and tone) can make or break you when you apologize or acknowledge. If the client believes you are just paying him/her lip service, you are in trouble before you begin.

The following is a call I took in 2001 and I happened to be taping myself that day. The call gives some further insight on the use of empathy and apologizing.

It is a warm spring day and the phone rings. Mike, one of the Cooper Pest customer service representatives answers the phone. He is greeted to by an angry client, who it turns out has been a client with us for 20 years.

The client is furious we missed an appointment, and is demanding to speak with me. The client has seen our WOW mission on our service orders along with a statement regarding our commitment to achieving the WOW standard. Mike calls my office and gives me the name of the client, Marcel Bouvant and transfers the call. It is important to remember the rule of first names as I begin the call. Mr. Bouvant has not given me permission to use his first name yet and since I know Mr. Bouvant is on the phone I should not ask his name. Therefore, I begin with addressing the client as Mr. Bouvant:

Phil: *Hello Mr. Bouvant, this is Phillip Cooper, Mike has explained the problem to me, can I recap what I know so far?*

Marcel: *Yes you may.*

Phil: *According to Mike, you had to wait over 40 minutes past your appointment for our technician to arrive at your home and it has wreaked havoc with your day.*

Marcel: *That is correct*

Now the empathy is important.

Phil: *Mr. Bouvant, I agree that you should be upset and if it were me I would be angrier than you are now. It simply is not acceptable for us to make an appointment and not be there on time. I am sure you had other things to do besides sitting around waiting for us? Is that a fair statement?*

Marcel: *Yes, I did have other things to do besides wait around all morning for your tech to show up.*

Phil: *Mr. Bouvant I know that I value my time at over $200 per hour, do you have an estimate of how much your time is worth, to help me determine how much we cost you?*

Marcel: *I am not really sure, does it matter?*

Phil: *To me it does, because by wasting your time, we took you away from doing activities that you could have been doing. Is that a fair statement?*

I actually could come up with other ways to empathize and this is only one example. Ultimately, my goal is for Mr. Bouvant to understand that I do appreciate the problem we caused and I care about his pain. Empathy is a powerful tool to use when the other party is upset.

Putting WOW to work only begins with empathy; once the client has given a wealth of information I am ready to find opportunities to WOW and I do this through asking questions. Asking questions is the soul mate of listening, and to fix the problem we need information which forces us to ask questions. We are back to the WOW system. Opportunities are everywhere during problem resolution in each problem there is a WOW moment begging to happen. We simply need to ask a bunch of questions to understand why the client is upset and to listen to what the client is saying. We then process this information with our strong product knowledge to provide solutions so we can fix the problem. Then we have the opportunity to go beyond what the client would expect, and we can grab the WOW moment.

Problem resolution reared its head on July 19, 2003 and this time we simply did not keep our appointment at the client's home. In less than 10 pages, I have shown two missed appointments and while they are good examples, this is not a common occurrence at Cooper, but they make for great examples when it does happen. Missing an appointment is simply customer unfriendly and we have many systems in place that prevent this from happening. Remember the expression, "To Err is Human, To Recover is Divine." Once again we were human.

In this case, the failure at Cooper was internal and created a very unhappy client. When the smoke cleared we determined the mistake occurred when the appointment was scheduled by the client. During that conversation, our customer service representative had accidentally scheduled the service under the wrong date, and our client wasted an entire morning waiting for our technician to appear. Unfortunately, I did not have a tape of the conversation. I often wonder how well we summarized and concluded on this phone call. A rule at Cooper is, all computer entry involved with scheduling should be done before the summary and conclusion so when we are summarizing the appointment, we are reading the information that is on the monitor. If that process had been followed 100 percent, I suspect we would have caught the mistake during the summary step. The bottom line was the appointment was not in our computer on the correct day.

The appointment was between 8 and 11 am and around 12:15 Mrs. Ferster called our office. When I took the call she was frustrated about losing her morning. I apologized for the error and employed empathy. Once the apology was given, Mrs. Ferster wanted to schedule the appointment for the following Saturday. I stopped and asked her if I could ask a few questions, before I went ahead and scheduled the service. As I started to ask the questions I was looking for specific information and it centered on finding a time that would be convenient for her and would make her life easy. I already knew she had been inconvenienced, and it was my turn to extend Cooper Pest Control to fix the problem and I was searching for WOW opportunities. The questions I asked were:

Phil: *Mrs. Ferster, can you share with me your schedule for the upcoming week?*

Mrs. Ferster:	*Please call me Beverly. I work during the week and do not get home until after 5:00 p.m. I know you do not schedule appointments after 5 p.m.*
Phil:	*If we were to come after 5 p.m. is there a better day for you?*
Mrs. Ferster:	*Most days would be fine.*
Phil:	*If I were to schedule an exact appointment which would you prefer, a Saturday or a weekday after work?*
Mrs. Ferster:	*I did not think you scheduled exact appointments.*
Phil:	*Well, as you know our minimum time range is two hours, but we have already wasted your entire Saturday morning so I would be more than happy to schedule an exact appointment at your convenience.*
Mrs. Ferster:	*That is really not necessary, but I appreciate your concern, a week night would be better.*
Phil:	*Then can we schedule the service for this Tuesday for 5:15p.m. to give you a bit of time to get home?*
Mrs. Ferster:	*That would be great.*

Now did I WOW Beverly, well that is hard to say. At the very least, I did achieve the by-product of outstanding customer service. But what happened next took this right to WOW. On, Tuesday evening I received an e-mail from Mrs. Ferster:

Hi Phil,

I had spoken with you on Saturday, July 19, when the technician did not come for monthly service. You were very accommodating by scheduling service for today, Tuesday, July 22 at 5:15 p.m. Many people (including myself) call to complain about service (as above) and *often do not take the time to praise service. I would like to compliment you for today. I've heard through the years that if a person is unhappy with something they will tell 75 people; if they are satisfied they will tell 25 people. I wonder why that is . . . .*

First, thanks again for scheduling my call after work. Second, there was a very bad thunderstorm late this afternoon, including hail. I had planned on leaving work before 5 p.m., but wasn't able to because of the storm. On my way home it started raining again and I was caught in traffic. Ron, my regular technician, was just turning the truck around to leave as I pulled up. It was about 5:30 p.m. He patiently waited for me to get in the house

I definitely would have to call this WOW service!

I had thanked Ron and told him about the error in my scheduling, for the previous Saturday, and how accommodating you had been. He told me how hard you work to satisfy customers and that your company has been the best to work for.

Just think, I was late this time and he actually waited for me!

I commend you on your customer service! I have been in the service industry my entire professional life. I have always treated people the way I would like to be treated. This is the first time I can recall receiving that kind of treatment!

> *Thank you!*
> *Sincerely,*
> *Beverly Ferster*

P.S. Ron told me he was leaving, he will be sorely missed! He is personable, professional and accommodating.

There were some things that occurred the day that Ron our technician went to the Fersters' to allow the recovery to continue. To begin with on his work order were detailed notes about what occurred to this point and this was important as Ron knew we were already in a problem resolution situation. With his senses heightened and knowing she was scheduled for an exact time, but also realizing that the weather might delay the arrival of Mrs. Ferster, he made the judgment call to wait and knew there was an opportunity to continue the recovery process from the original error.

Ultimately, when it comes to problem resolution you need to be on the top of your WHAT + HOW game. It takes a lot of practice to be able to handle those problem calls and turn them into WOW moments, but once you have, the recovery is divine!

CHAPTER 22

WOW Your Teammates

I want to conclude this book with a quick introspective of how WOW has transformed Cooper Pest Control and how other organizations have embraced the concept WOW at Cooper Pest Control goes beyond the WHAT + HOW system, it is our culture. The WOW concepts permeate the organization at all levels and have allowed us to achieve growth levels once thought unimaginable while increasing our profitably. We have an organization that knows how to have fun and works hard to push the company forward everyday. What we do at Cooper with WOW is what WOW is all about and why I believe so strongly in the system.

When developing the mission for Cooper Pest Control, I decided it needed to be simple and known to all. As part of our cultural overhaul in 1999, we changed our mission to meet my requirements. Before '99, the mission for Cooper Pest Control was close to 250 words. I actually loved our mission and it was developed with great care, but this was before I recognized that it was too long. I had looked at the missions of many large corporations that I admired and in 1990 came up with the Cooper mission. The problem was that no one in our organization could recite it back. It is no surprise that no one could even paraphrase it correctly.

The mission throughout the nineties was:

Cooper Pest Control offers a wide array of pest control services and products to our residential and commercial clients. We are committed to delivering these services in an ethical and professional manner with safety for our customers and the environment as a primary concern.

We view our employees as individuals with unique needs and personal goals. Employees can expect security, compassion, hands on experience, and technical training, along with the knowledge that they are a part of a team committed to excellence and success. We provide employees with opportunities for growth and advancement.

Our commitment to quality is our guiding force, with client satisfaction being our number one priority. We only offer quality products and services in a timely fashion. In all situations, exceeding our client's expectations is our goal.

We promote and assist the pest control industry in its efforts through participation in the State and National trade organizations. We are active in the pest control trade association's committees in our effort to make the industry stronger.

The health and welfare of the communities that we serve are very important and are directly tied to our success. We strive to broaden public awareness of the benefits of pest control, to include the development of educational tools that we present to schools.

Our final commitment is to continually research new technologies and methods of delivering service that focuses on reducing exposure to pesticides and offering pesticide free alternatives as a solution to pest management problems. Our efforts should result in being recognized by the industry as a visionary and dynamic company, which is an industry leader in providing cutting edge pest control services.

As part of the cultural transformation in the year 2000 our mission changed. It is simple and everyone in the organization knows it and can repeat it.

> ➤ *WOW our Clients*
> ➤ *WOW our Teammates*
> ➤ *WOW our Community*
> ➤ *WOW our Service Partners*
> ➤ *WOW our Bottom Line*

The mission is only the beginning of WOW at Cooper. WOW does not happen with the implementation of a mission, it must permeate throughout the organization. During my visit to Commerce, John Manning told of how often competitors try to imitate WOW, however, Commerce understands that by instituting some of the Commerce WOW ideas, WOW will not occur. It takes a paradigm shift, a cultural change in the entire organization to create a WOW culture.

This is not to be construed with the goal of honing the skills of customer service professionals. As we have explored through the book, a customer service professional must hone their skills through practice and that is why we have, WHAT + HOW. Instead, what I am discussing here is the company culture and the organizational shift to a WOW system.

If you decide to bring the WOW concepts into your organization I strongly believe that picking an idea here and there simply will not work. WOW needs to permeate throughout the organization in everything you do. Whether you call it WOW or something else, the bottom line is that everything that the company does must all begin and end with the WOW concepts being maintained and encouraged. As we developed the WOW concepts within Cooper Pest Control I focused on the second line of our mission, WOW your teammates. It takes on great importance, the acknowledgement that you must WOW your teammates. WHAT + HOW is not just about communicating to our clients, but it also involves communicating with our teammates.

To the end of creating the WOW atmosphere I began instituting a number of programs to emphasize WOW and we continually look for more. Every other month we have a WOW lunch where we gather our inside staff to celebrate WOW. Each lunch a separate department is in charge of picking the food theme and getting the lunch, but when the food is displayed before the vultures hit the table the food must spell the word WOW. We have had Italian Hot Dog WOW, BBQ WOW, Chinese WOW, you name it and my teammates find more ingenuitive ways to spell WOW. At the lunch we set WOW goals for each team and give bonuses based on the successes of our teams and the company in achieving short term and long term goals. The lunch is fun, but if forces the mindset that WOW is important and is critical to our success.

Each month, we gather our entire organization, (in 2003 approximately 50 people) for a staff meeting. The conclusion of every meeting is WOW dollars. I go around the room and ask if anyone knows of an instance where we succeeded in our mission in the past 30 days the teammate tells the story and I hand out $10 to the person who achieved WOW. I also come armed with notes from our clients and audio tape of clients who have left messages in the past 30 days of WOW moments. Yes, I get at least two calls per week from HAPPY external clients along with countess notes from

WOWed clients. Before the year 2000, I could count on one hand the number of calls or notes I would receive in a year. Now the numbers keep increasing monthly.

What I love the best during our WOW dollars are teammates recognizing other teammates for things they have done to WOW one another. Is $10 a large sum of money, absolutely not, but it is the recognition and pride that is most important. Once in a while, someone will haul in $30 or so and there is a lot of ribbing from teammates.

Once in a while I have to reign the troops in, to insure that WOW continues to be WOW. In early '2003, we promoted some member of the team into manager positions to accommodate our increasing growth. During the first three months of '2003, these new managers were receiving WOWs from their teammates at an increasing rate. Some of the WOWs they were receiving were part of their standard duties and it was their teammates' attempts at impressing their new managers. For the first two months I let it go, I felt it was important for the managers to be recognized in their new positions and I know that the first two months had positive impact.

In March, after the first couple months of WOWs to these new managers, I made a comment that many of the WOWs the managers were doing were part of their daily function. Going forward we were raising the bar and if a manager was going to be recognized for a WOW moment it needed to be extraordinary and in line with the definition that it was discussed at the dinner table with family or friends.

Two weeks later, Stuart one of our newer teammates approached me. "Phil, I wanted to WOW John (his manager) at the next staff meeting, but I know what you said. Let me tell you what he did and can you tell me if it was WOW. I was looking at how John arranged the inside of his truck and was very impressed and asked him if he could help me. Not only did he help, but he came over to my house last Sunday on his day off and worked with me for 3 hours." A big smile came over my face and with great pleasure I replied, "A WOW that is." This is what WOW is about and as important is the recognition by staff that WOWing the internal client, the teammate, is critical to the success of our organization.

WOW is entrenched within the culture of Cooper and everyone in the organization is involved. We have fun with it, but we also remember that we need to practice WOW everyday and I am proud of my team and how they carry it out. Interestingly, Cooper is not alone with a WOW program. Commerce Bank, one of my favorite companies around has their own WOW program that is simply outstanding.

Commerce Bank

In New Jersey, we have one of the success stories in the business world brewing, Commerce Bank. This bank also has acknowledged that the State of Customer Service in general has much to be desired. Commerce, has taken most of the rules and traditions of banking and thrown them out the door. What they have developed is a culture and new standards for an industry that delivered average customer service.

When you look at Commerce you must start with their leader Vernon W. Hill II. Mr. Hill founded the bank in 1973 at the age of 26. As a graduate of the University of Pennsylvania's Wharton School of Business, he had the vision of creating a bank that thought different, looked different and provided a totally different banking experience for customers. "When we started Commerce, it was clear the world didn't need another 'me too' bank,'" Mr. Hill noted. He has served as the Chairman and President of Commerce Bancorp, Inc.

since the opening of the first branch in Marlton, New Jersey.

Mr. Hill's ability to combine a retail business strategy with a passion for providing customers with WOW! service that is unsurpassed has been instrumental in Commerce Bank's dynamic success. Mr. Hill was named Bank CEO Of The Year for 2003 by US Banker Magazine and one of the top five CEOs of all businesses for 2002 by Investor's Business Daily newspaper.

As "America's Most Convenient Bank," Commerce has developed a unique banking model in the tradition of America's great retailers such as Home Depot, Wal-Mart and Starbucks.

From its original location with 9 employees, to nearly 270 stores in 4 states, with more than 8,900 employees, Commerce is recognized as a true American growth story.

Like Cooper Pest, Commerce celebrates the WOW moments of both internal and external clients, but they take it to a whole other level. Commerce has a WOW department devoted to delivering the WOW message and processing the inbound traffic generated from their WOW message. This department spends its entire day devoted to building the WOW culture within Commerce.

Commerce offers many incentives for WOWing Customers. One incentive program has employees collecting little red stickers in the shape of the Commerce C Logo. Employees who WOW! Customers are given stickers later redeemed for Fun Commerce Prizes.

Employees are also eligible to nominate each other for quarterly WOW! Awards by sending in stories of WOW! Customer service they've observed. Winners are surprised with a visit from the WOW! Patrol. Picture a WOW! van pulling up in front of your building. The doors pop open and a pack of cheering co-workers jumps out, runs into your office and presents you with a WOW Cash Reward!

Just when you thought that was enough, all Commerce employees gather together each year to celebrate the best of the best WOWers of the previous year. They call it the WOW! Awards. This year, the annual celebration was held at the world-renowned Radio City Music Hall in New York City. 8000 employees packed the theatre to cheer for over 200 nominees of various awards. Best Part Time Teller, Best Retail Support, Best Call Center Representative, and many others. One lucky person each year is the recipient of the Chairman's Award for Service Excellence. This year's winner drove away in a brand new Red Porsche. WOW!

Being a fan of Commerce I decided to learn more about their organization and learned that WOW begins when you are hired at Commerce. All new hires attend a full day session titled "Traditions". The Commerce Model is built on Service. Commerce Traditions is built around the delivery of just that message. Each new hire completes this class on their first day as a means of Protecting the Culture and Building the Brand and Having some Fun!"

Commerce understands what WOW is about and they live it everyday. It is allowing them to develop one of the more unique banking cultures in the country and their vision of WOW is right on the mark.

Contented Cows Give Better Milk

One of my favorite books is "Contented Cows Give Better Milk," written by Bill Catlette and Richard Hadden. The book is all about having employees that are content, "the cows" and the direct result is increased growth and profits "the milk." The authors look at a variety of companies that have invested into culture and their employees and the resulting return on investment. This book is another you should add to your "must read" list and they also have a great website, www.contentedcows.com. Most of the companies they examine have put in place a culture similar to WOW where the teammates simply go the extra mile. The book examines some of the premier companies in the country and how the investment pays off. The bottom line is that WOW is an investment that has a tremendous rate on return when implemented effectively.

Putting it all together—
Patrick Bodden, Advance Realty

To understand the power of WOW you need to go no further than Advance Realty and look at the affect WOW has had on Patrick Bodden.

In May 2002, I had just completed a training session for Advance Realty with their management team. They learned the WOW doctrines and were now putting them to use. Patrick Bodden is one of the Advance managers in Massachusetts and he was working with one of their tenants. As soon as he returned to his office he composed an e-mail to a potential client Advance was courting for leased space. I include this e-mail as a way to see how WOW can become part of all of your communication. The e-mail elicited such a tremendous response that it was forwarded to me as an example of how WOW was transforming the thinking at Advance. Patrick put all of WOW together in a brief e-mail and scored! What is even more exciting is the e-mail I received from Patrick in December 2003, describing the ongoing effect of WOW. I sent some material for Patrick to preview before this book went to print and his e-mail response was a testimony to what WOW can do. When WOW is put to work the affects are tremendous and they impact Patrick Bodden to this day.

—Original Message—

From: Patrick Bodden
Sent: Friday, May 10, 2002 3:06 PM
To: xxxxxx
Subject: Westboro Executive Park

Don:

It was a pleasure meeting you and Robert the other day regarding the potential lease at 112 Turnpike Road. I hope you find that our facility meets, <company's name> requirements. I wanted to compliment you on your response to my statement that Advance Realty Group is committed to providing customer service to it's tenants beyond the norm to which you asked, "How". This was not a question I've been asked before and quite frankly I was disappointed with my response and was obviously not as prepared as I should have been. This missed opportunity has bothered me since our meeting, so I wanted to follow up and answer your question properly.

It is my company's belief that a primary measure of our success is customer satisfaction. We spend a lot of time at all management levels insuring that this is delivered to our tenants by not only providing the best possible work environment but also the way we deliver our services. Our onsite staff is trained to conduct themselves professionally and friendlily, we constantly survey our performance so that it can be internally evaluated and improvements made, we expect to surprise our tenants with our responsiveness and creativity, we look for ways to help with our tenant's business success beyond the requirements of the lease.

Some examples of this are the new amenities that I explained during your tour and the Naked Fish gift certificate. In addition, we have ordered complimentary umbrellas that beginning next month we intend to loan our tenants on rainy days, we recognize our appreciation for your tenancy on each lease anniversary and make a point to meet with our tenants to discuss their needs, we follow up with phone calls upon completion of tenant work orders to be sure your needs were met promptly and thoroughly. We host some creative events throughout the year which add pleasant conveniences, breaks from the day to day routine and develop a sense of community among the tenants. Our goal is to make your decision to renew your lease at the end of the initial term easy because of this value added service.

We know that you have many real estate options these days, service is our passion and we feel that this sets Advance Realty Group apart from our competitors. I would be happy to provide you with some tenant references who have offered to explain their improved experience since we purchased the property in December of 2000.

For your convenience I have attached a PDF of the suite you were interested in.

Please feel free to contact me if you would like another tour or have any questions. I hope you'll choose to pursue a lease at Westboro Executive Park and take advantage of the added benefits and conveniences we offer.

Patrick S. Bodden
Regional Property Manager
Advance Realty Group

The follow-up e-mail December 2003

—Original Message—

From: Patrick Bodden
Sent: Monday, December 01, 2003 3:12 PM
To: Phillip D. Cooper
Cc: Kurt Padavano
Subject: RE: Patrick Bodden Passage

That is very cool, can't wait to get my copy. Please let me know when it is published.

I think that that e-mail was only the very beginning and an inspiration of a now much expanded marketing process where I now seek out ways like that to have direct follow up with prospective tenants after the initial showing. I have had many positive responses from these prospects, including the word WOW, usually followed by, "You're the only property manager who's taken the time to spend with me out of all the buildings we've toured".

Phil, We have had uncanny success in leasing here since I wrote that e-mail where we've watched the local market continue to decline while our leasing has increased. We're not selling anything different than anybody else except customer service. We have evidence of our competitors copying many of our techniques but they don't know how to put it all together like we do thanks to your little presentation in Philly. Not every successful lease can be attributed to our Customer Service but many have been positively influenced by it and some can absolutely be attributed to this alone.

So thanks a lot not only for the book reference but also for the skill and inspiration to do my job better.

Patrick Bodden
Regional Property Manager
Advance Realty Group

Implementing WOW is what it is all about. Taping, grading, role playing, incorporating the WOW concepts into e-mail; they all play an important role. By taking it to hear you too can be ready for Game Day just like Patrick!

A WOW to all and to all a Good Night

WOW! It's a very simple concept that can transform you and your organization. To produce those WOW moments to hit the grand slam, to WOW your teammates or your clients, you must remember to practice. I hope you use the concepts of this book to change the way you go about your daily business. Life can be so much fun as we strive to WOW. The feeling when we hit a WOW moment well it is a WOW! Remember it is all about WHAT YOU COMMUNICATE and HOW YOU COMMUNICATE and with some work you will achieve those WOW moments!

APPENDIX

Quick Grading Reference
(reprint from earlier in the book)

Tips for Grading

A**s you begin to grade yourself, the following are
some quick tips to consider when grading each of the
items; you will find a copy of this in the appendix
section, Quick Grading Reference.

WHAT To Communicate

Excellent Product Knowledge

- Did your statements match up with company
  collateral regarding the product/or service you
  were speaking about?
- Did you remember all of the important items
  about the product?
- Were there things about the product that you
  should have been discussed in the conversation?
- Were you clear in your descriptions of the
  product?
- Was there any other product knowledge that
  could have prompted other questions/

- Were you able to integrate any other technology (computer etc) without affecting the call?
- Be sure to have this area cross graded to insure that your knowledge of the product was appropriate.

Communication of Expectations

- Does the client know what to expect?

Clear presentation of the options

- Were too many options presented?
- Were any options presented?
- Did the client understand the options being given?
- Be sure to have this area cross graded to insure you presented the proper options.

Only communicate what is needed to make a decision

- Was anything communicated that posed an issue where one did not exist?

Documentation

- Did you find opportunities to provide items in writing to the client?
- Did you document the call well with well written notes for others to refer to?

HOW to Communicate

Exude Confidence

- Was confidence oozing out of you?

- Did you hide behind policies or company procedure (bad confidence/black sticky tar)?

Customer Friendly

- Was the conversation like speaking with a neighbor?
- Did the call have a rhythm to it?
- Were their any unfriendlies in the conversation (unauthorized hold, excessive hold, patronizing the other party, etc.)?
- What Customer Friendly things did you do?

Smile Factor

- Were you smiling during the conversation?
- Did you use body language during the communication that was positive in nature?

Pace

- How was the beginning of the conversation, a neutral pace is important to show that you are not rushed, good speed, inflection and tone to create positive first impression
- Was the speed of the conversation at a speed which the listener could understand?
- Did the speed of the words have a rhythm, at times faster at times slower?
- Did you inflect on the words bringing them to life?
- Did you use tone that was positive in nature?

Enunciation

- Could the other party clearly understand what you were saying?

Pronouns

- Did you avoid the use of four letter word of customer service, THEY?
- Did you emphasize I, we, us, and you?
- Did you reference teammate's names or department names?

Names

- Did you follow the rules of your organization as it relates to the use of first vs. last names?
- Did you pronounce the name correctly throughout the conversation?
- Did you say the name at the beginning of the conversation?
- Did you say the name at the end of the conversation?
- If the call was more than 90 seconds, did you use the 90 second rule and mix in the name additional times?
- Did you overuse the name during the conversation?

Ask Questions

- Did you ask questions during the conversation?
- Did you employ the 30/70 rule? (if you spoke more than 30 percent of the time, you probably did not ask enough questions)?
- Have someone cross grade this for you to see if there were opportunities for other questions that you did not raise.

Listen

- Did you employ the 30/70 rule and listen 70 percent of the time?

- Did you hear everything the client said?
- Did you have to re-ask any information due to not hearing the client correctly the first time?

Avoid the Use of Jargon

- Were any words used that the receiving party did not understand?
- Did the receiving party become confused at any point during the conversation?

Warm and Fuzzies

- Did you use adjectives?
- Did you use anecdotes?
- Did you use empathy?
- If you used adjectives, anecdotes or empathy was the client's reaction positive?

Summarize and Conclude

- Was a precise summary provided at the end of the conversation highlighting the major points of the communication?
- Did you conclude with, "{name} is there anything else I can do for you today?"

Our Way From Gale

reprinted with permission The Gale Co.

Gale
"Can Do"

The Gale Company Winning Attitude

Their Way	Our Way
We've never done it before	We have the opportunity to be the first
It's too complicated	Let's look at it from a different angle
We don't have the resources	Necessity is the mother of invention
It will never work	**Let's give it a try**
There's not enough time	We'll reevaluate some priorities
We already tried it	We learn from experience
There's no way it'll work	**We can make it work**
It's a waste of time	Think of the possibilities
It's a waste of money	The investment will be worth it
We don't have the expertise	Let's network with those who do
We can't compete	**We'll get a jump on the competition**
Our vendors won't go for it	Let's show them the opportunity
It's good enough	There's always room for improvement
We're understaffed	We're a lean mean machine!
We don't have enough room	Temporary space may be an option
It will never fly	We'll never know until we try
We don't have the equipment	Maybe we can sub it out
It's not going to be any better	We'll try it one more time
It can't be done	**It can be done**
No one communicates	Let's open the channels
Isn't it time to go home?	Days go so quickly around here!
I don't have any idea	I'll come up with some alternatives
Let somebody else deal with it	I'm ready to learn something new
We're always changing direction	We're in touch with our customers
It's too radical a change	**Let's take a chance**
It takes too long for approval	We'll walk it through the system
Our customers won't buy it	We'll educate them
Our company is the wrong size	We're perfect for this project
It doesn't fit us	We should look at it
It's contrary to policy	**Anything's possible**
It's not my job	I'll be glad to take the responsibility
WE CAN'T	**WE CAN**

Grading Sheet with disclaimer on use

WHAT + HOW GRADING SHEET

What + How = WOW.
c/o Cooper Pest Solutions
351 Lawrence Station Road
Lawrenceville, NJ 08648
(800) 949-2687
phil.cooper@cooperpest.com
www.whatplushow.com

CSR Name _____

Cross Grader Name _____

Caller Name _____

Date _____

ITEM	Self Grade	Cross Grade	COMMENTS
Product Knowledge			
Excellent product knowledge	1 2 3 4 5 6 7 8 9 10	1 2 3 4 5 6 7 8 9 10	
Communication of Expectations	1 2 3 4 5 6 7 8 9 10	1 2 3 4 5 6 7 8 9 10	
Clear presentation of the options	1 2 3 4 5 6 7 8 9 10	1 2 3 4 5 6 7 8 9 10	
Only communicate what the prospect/client needs to make a decision	1 2 3 4 5 6 7 8 9 10	1 2 3 4 5 6 7 8 9 10	
Being able to provide written support material to back up your conversation	1 2 3 4 5 6 7 8 9 10	1 2 3 4 5 6 7 8 9 10	
How to communicate			
Exude confidence	1 2 3 4 5 6 7 8 9 10	1 2 3 4 5 6 7 8 9 10	
Customer-friendly CSR process	1 2 3 4 5 6 7 8 9 10	1 2 3 4 5 6 7 8 9 10	
SMILE Factor	1 2 3 4 5 6 7 8 9 10	1 2 3 4 5 6 7 8 9 10	
Pace	1 2 3 4 5 6 7 8 9 10	1 2 3 4 5 6 7 8 9 10	
Enunciation	1 2 3 4 5 6 7 8 9 10	1 2 3 4 5 6 7 8 9 10	
Proper use of pronouns (I, we, they)	1 2 3 4 5 6 7 8 9 10	1 2 3 4 5 6 7 8 9 10	
Reference to prospect/clients name (at least 2x)	1 2 3 4 5 6 7 8 9 10	1 2 3 4 5 6 7 8 9 10	
Ask questions	1 2 3 4 5 6 7 8 9 10	1 2 3 4 5 6 7 8 9 10	
Listen	1 2 3 4 5 6 7 8 9 10	1 2 3 4 5 6 7 8 9 10	
Avoid Jargon	1 2 3 4 5 6 7 8 9 10	1 2 3 4 5 6 7 8 9 10	
Warm & Fuzzies	1 2 3 4 5 6 7 8 9 10	1 2 3 4 5 6 7 8 9 10	
Summarize & Conclude	1 2 3 4 5 6 7 8 9 10	1 2 3 4 5 6 7 8 9 10	

ITEM	Self Grade	Cross Grade	COMMENTS
Overall Objectives			
Did you WOW the Client The Overall Grade	1 2 3 4 5 6 7 8 9 10	1 2 3 4 5 6 7 8 9 10	
Did you Increase level of customer satisfaction?	1 2 3 4 5 6 7 8 9 10	1 2 3 4 5 6 7 8 9 10	
Did you insure that they want to use us now and in the future?	1 2 3 4 5 6 7 8 9 10	1 2 3 4 5 6 7 8 9 10	
Does the client perceive value in working with us?	1 2 3 4 5 6 7 8 9 10	1 2 3 4 5 6 7 8 9 10	
Do you understand the prospect/client's needs?	1 2 3 4 5 6 7 8 9 10	1 2 3 4 5 6 7 8 9 10	
Did you determine the most appropriate products/services based on their needs?	1 2 3 4 5 6 7 8 9 10	1 2 3 4 5 6 7 8 9 10	
Does our clients understand their options?	1 2 3 4 5 6 7 8 9 10	1 2 3 4 5 6 7 8 9 10	
Does our clients know the various products and services we offer?	1 2 3 4 5 6 7 8 9 10	1 2 3 4 5 6 7 8 9 10	
Did you find Opportunities to increase value, business opportunities, sales, and level of customer satisfaction?	1 2 3 4 5 6 7 8 9 10	1 2 3 4 5 6 7 8 9 10	
Did you develop client's trust in YOU?	1 2 3 4 5 6 7 8 9 10	1 2 3 4 5 6 7 8 9 10	

WHAT + HOW = WOW

c/o Cooper Pest Solutions
351 Lawrence Station Road
Lawrenceville, NJ 08648
(800) 949-2667
phil.cooper@cooperpest.com
www.whatplushow.com

WHAT & HOWä INSTRUCTION GUIDE

I. Equipment Required

1. Radio Shack Cassette Tape Recorder

   A. Model CTR-122
   B. Catalog # 14-1129
   C. Voice activated—do not substitute with lesser model

2. Radio Shack Mini Record Control

   A. Catalog # 43-1237

   B. Radio Shack equipment can be purchased on line at http://www.radioshack.com

3. Telephone

II. Setup Procedure

1. To set up recorder and a phone

   A. Unplug the handset cord from the telephone (not the end plugged to the receiver).

   B. Plug in open jack of handset just removed into the Radio Shack Mini Record Control.

   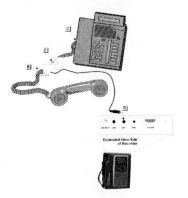

   C. Plug in open jack from Radio Shack Mini Record Control (small coiled cord which is part of the unit) into the phone where you removed the handset cord.

   D. On the same side of the Radio Shack Mini Record Control there is a jack that plugs into the "mic" labeled input on side of recorder.

E. On Radio Shack Mini Record Control, there is a switch which must be set to REC (far left).

F. Pause Button (located on top of recorder) should be set to OFF position

G. AC Adapter vs. Batteries

  a) You can try the AC Adapter, but it is likely that you will encounter a buzz on the phone. If this occurs, you will need to use batteries ONLY (2 AA batteries required).

2. Settings for Radio Shack Optimus Cassette Tape Recorder

  A. On back of recorder you will see 3 switches which must be set to the following settings. This will allow the voice activation to function correctly.

  a) VOX (Tone): HIGH (In) [far left position]
  b) MIC SENSITIVITY: MEDIUM (middle position)
  c) TAPE SPEED: NORMAL (middle position)

3. Start up at beginning of day

  A. The settings on the recorder are designed to take advantage of the voice activation feature. You should not touch the recorder until the tape runs out. It will start and stop automatically when you begin your telephone conversations.

B.   Insure that pause button in is off position.

C.   Push the Record Button (this button is marked and has a red dot on it).

4.   End of day

A.   You must push the Stop button on the recorder.

a)   If you do not do this, the batteries will run out.

I. Equipment Required

1. Radio Shack Cassette Tape Recorder

    A. Model CTR-122
    B. Catalog # 14-1129
    C. Voice activated—do not substitute with lesser model

2. Radio Shack Mini Record Control

    A. Approximate Cost: $14.99
    B. Catalog # 43-1237

    C. Radio Shack equipment can be purchased on line at http://www.radioshack.com

3. Telephone

4. Plantronics 900 MHz Cordless Belt Pack with Headset (CS10)

    A. Catalog # 1769

    B. Can be purchased on line through Hello Direct at http://www.hellodirect.com

II. Setup Procedure

1. To set up recorder and a phone

    A. Unplug the handset cord from the telephone (not the end plugged to the receiver).

    B. Plug in open jack of handset just removed into the Radio Shack Mini Record Control.

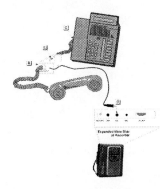

C. Plug in open jack from Radio Shack Mini Record Control (small coiled cord which is part of the unit) into the phone where you removed the handset cord.

D. On the same side of the Radio Shack Mini Record Control there is a jack that plugs into the "mic" labeled input on side of recorder.

E. On Radio Shack Mini Record Control, there is a switch which must be set to REC (far left).

F. Pause Button (located on top of recorder) should be set to OFF position

G. AC Adapter vs. Batteries

a) You can try the AC Adapter, but it is likely that you will encounter a buzz on the phone. If this occurs, you will need to use batteries ONLY (2 AA batteries required).

H. Begin with instructions listed above until you have the short end of phone cord coming from "rec/play" switch. That end of cord will be plugged into the

amplifier where you see the small symbol
of a telephone that has a phone jack below
it. The amplifier will be plugged into wall.
The handset will need to be lifted from the
base in order to hear dial tone unless phone
is programmed with "release" key

2. Settings for Radio Shack Optimus Cassette Tape
Recorder

   A. On back of recorder you will see 3
   switches which must be set to the
   following settings. This will allow the
   voice activation to function correctly.

      a) VOX (Tone): HIGH (In) [far left
      position]
      b) MIC SENSITIVITY: MEDIUM (middle
      position)
      c) TAPE SPEED: NORMAL (middle
      position)

3. Start up at beginning of day

   A. The settings on the recorder are designed
   to take advantage of the voice activation
   feature. You should not touch the
   recorder until the tape runs out. It will
   start and stop automatically when you
   begin your telephone conversations.
   B. Insure that pause button in is off position.

TOP VIEW OF RECORDER

C. Push the Record Button (this button is marked and has a red dot on it).

TOP VIEW OF RECORDER

4. End of day

   A. You must push the Stop button on the recorder.

      a) If you do not do this, the batteries will run out.